ENGRAVED GEMS

The Ionides Collection

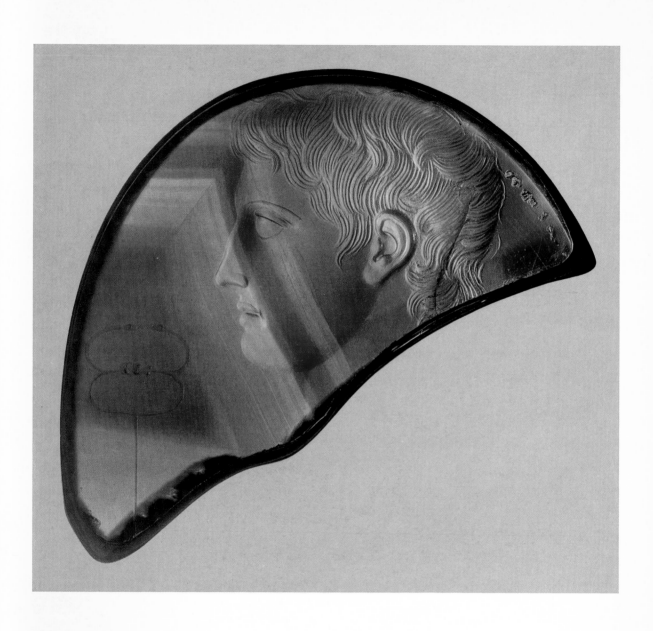

ENGRAVED GEMS

The Ionides Collection

JOHN BOARDMAN

photographs by

ROBERT L. WILKINS

NORTHWESTERN UNIVERSITY PRESS · EVANSTON

1968

Library of Congress Catalog Card Number: 68-17325

© 1968 THAMES AND HUDSON LONDON
PRINTED IN SWITZERLAND BY DRUCKEREI WINTERTHUR AG

Contents

CHAPTER I

Introduction

Of all the arts of Classical antiquity that of gem-engraving is the one which survived the Middle Ages the least altered and the best appreciated. The techniques
and materials of Renaissance engravers in Italy and France were those of the Greeks
and Romans. The forms and often the subjects of the gems were strongly in-
fluenced by Classical models. Roman gems and cameos were themselves often
mounted on crosses, caskets, crowns and book-bindings, despite their pagan motifs.
In Renaissance Italy, Roman gems were collected by connoisseurs and artists, they
were copied and they inspired new, classicizing works in a very similar style. With
the growth of scholarly expertise, the skill and artistry of the copyist improved
until, in the eighteenth century, we find skilled artists adapting and copying freely
the Classical gems in the royal or ducal cabinets. In England it was the Earl of
Arundel who, in the early seventeenth century, made a major collection of Classical
and later gems, as he did of other antiquities. His gems passed eventually into the
great Marlborough Collection at Blenheim, itself dispersed by sale in the last century. This is the type and pedigree of many of the major gem collections in Europe.

We have, however, to distinguish this connoisseur interest in Greek and Roman
gems, centred largely in the miniature perfection of their representations of myth
and portraiture, from the history of engraved gems as part of the history of Classical art. To demean them to the class of 'minor arts' betrays impatience with their
size and ignorance of the advanced techniques and accomplishment displayed by
the finest examples. To admire them only as a mirror in miniature of the 'major

9

arts' of sculpture and painting does scant justice to what was always a respected and highly individual art. In Greece, in particular, we find periods in which the repertory of subjects used by gem-engravers is quite different from that recorded in the other arts, while there are workshops which seem to have been exposed to influence and inspiration which left the other arts unmoved. In classical antiquity gem-engraving was unquestionably regarded as a major art, practised often by well-known sculptors or other artists whose names were honoured and remembered, unlike the names of vase-painters which we learn only from their surviving works.

In the history of Greek gems we can detect two periods of high achievement: the Late Archaic period of the generation before the Persian Wars, and the Late Hellenistic period, beginning in the capitals of Alexander's broken empire, especially at Alexandria in Egypt. In the first century BC, many of these Hellenistic artists came to Rome, attracted by a new patronage or obliged to serve it. There, in the Rome of the Late Republic and early Empire, of Caesar and Augustus, the culmination of their art was expressed in the portraiture and symbolic mythology of the scenes they cut on gems. It is the work of this period which occupies an important part of this book.

The intention of these chapters and photographs is to present, with brief narrative and description, the gems of the Ionides Collection in London. The collection itself, on which more will be found in Chapter VI, was made by C.A. Ionides, well known as benefactor of the Victoria and Albert Museum, and by his son, A.C. Ionides. It is now in the keeping of his great-grand-daughter, the Lady Adam Gordon, and her husband who have most generously and hospitably given the author and photographer free access to the gems. It is a small collection of some 120 pieces, but quite remarkable for its quality and particularly for its strength in gems of the Late Hellenistic and Early Roman period. Several pieces derive from the Arundel and Marlborough collections, already mentioned; others were acquired as other major collections came upon the market. A very few of the finer gems were known to Furtwängler when he wrote his classic *Die antiken Gemmen* at the end of the last century and some were exhibited in the Burlington Fine Art Club in 1903. But several more have escaped the detailed attention of connoisseurs and scholars, including important and signed works, while none of them have been accorded the sort of illustration which scholars and art historians of today require.

The early history of Classical gem-engraving, leading to the execution of these fine gems in Greece and Roman Italy, is sketched in the next chapter and illustrated also by prime examples from the same collection. It ranges from the work of an immigrant Greek artist in the sixth century BC, through specimens of the work of

Etruscan and Italic artists, to the Hellenistic Greek. The Roman gems and cameos are described in Chapters III and IV. And the account is completed in Chapter V with a selection of Late Renaissance and eighteenth-century gems which display the deceptive skill of the copyist as well as his considerable originality in handling classical themes. Fuller physical descriptions of the stones with reference to other relevant works or studies are given at the end of this book.

The photographs, by Robert L. Wilkins, are reproduced at four times the size of the stone, unless otherwise indicated. Viewing gems in enlargements of this size we are in danger of forgetting that this is essentially a miniaturist's art, that most of the pieces are no bigger than a finger-nail. But no life-size reproduction can do justice to the detail of the artist's work, and if the principle of enlargement for publication is accepted, it might as well be as great as the quality of the work will tolerate. Some details on these stones first became apparent to the writer only on these photographs. Yet there is no positive evidence that artists in antiquity used any magnifying aids. Perhaps ancient eyes enjoyed a finesse and clarity of vision which cannot normally be matched by modern eyes, jaded by the barrage of print to which they are subjected from tender years. Nowadays appreciation and execution of the miniature are the privilege of the machine-aided or the myopic.

Most of the Early Roman gems are illustrated only in the original stone, since they were probably cut to be viewed thus, no less than in impression. It may be observed, however, that although photographs of the concave intaglio on original stones can give the effect of relief, undue emphasis is then placed on the contour rather than the relief modelling, and this is particularly misleading when it is the mannered and less realistic conventions of Archaic art that are being reproduced. There are also, of course, gems of all periods whose material precludes successful photography of the original, because of their variety of colour, their preservation or the condition of setting. Almost all the Ionides gems are now set in modern gold rings, masked in the photographs.

The earlier scarabs shown here were cut principally for use in making impressions, and some photographs of impressions are therefore given as well as of originals. The later stones have where possible been lit from behind to exploit the translucency of the stone. When set as pendants in antiquity they could have been mounted without any backing so that they might be viewed in the same manner. It is note-worthy, however, that few ancient finger-rings have open bezels to allow this effect. They must have relied upon the light reflected from the surface or from a polished metal backing, and in the case of the domed 'carbuncles' [like *nos 41, 45*] to some degree upon oblique lighting. Pliny [*Natural History* xxxvii 31] recommends for certain sards either a gold- or silver-foil backing, and for topazes an open bezel or a foil of brass [ibid. 42]. Cameos generally require a backing since any lightening of the background strata through translucency diminishes the contrast with the pale surface layer, and destroys the effects of shallow cutting of this surface which is itself partly translucent. Transparent stones should be viewed by daylight, in the early morning, according to Pliny [ibid. 76]; and daylight, Ovid assures us [*Ars Amatoria* i 252f.], is required for the proper study of gems, as for dyed wool, and the faces and figures of young women.

CHAPTER II

Greek, Etruscan and Hellenistic Gems

The history of Classical gem-engraving begins in the second quarter of the sixth century BC. There had been, to be sure, important series of gems engraved in the Greek world before that date, such as the exquisite stones and gold rings of the Minoan and Mycenaean world; and in the eighth and seventh centuries BC there were new workshops cutting gems in soft stones or ivory, in styles which reflect various different aspects of Greek Geometric and Orientalizing art. But some time before the middle of the sixth century BC, new materials, techniques and forms were introduced to the Greek artist. These came from the East, apparently from Phoenicia and probably via Cyprus, where Greeks and Phoenicians lived side by side. The new materials were the hard stones of the chalcedony family, notably red cornelian. The new techniques were those required to work the harder stones, mainly the use of a cutting wheel and drill, probably driven by a bow, where before figures had been cut or gouged free-hand in the soft stone. The new form was the scarab seal, derived originally from Egypt. The body of the seal is in the form of a scarab beetle, while the flat oval underside bears the intaglio device. The stone is pierced lengthways so that it can be set on a swivel and worn as a pendant or as a finger-ring. In the latter case it would be worn with the beetle back facing out and, when needed for use as a signet, it could be taken off, and the stone turned to reveal the personal device.

For the next seventy-five years, Archaic Greek artists – principally, it seems, in the islands and East Greece, including Cyprus – lavished their best skills on these

13

miniature works. They soon lost interest in the beetle back to the scarab, rendering it in a summary fashion and often giving it a distinctive and anatomically inaccurate ridge along its spine, which copies a rare Phoenician usage. Some of the early workshops, however, treated the beetle with care, detailing the head and legs and adding another anatomical folly in the form of winglets incised on the outside of the beetle's wing cases. This was also a period in which East Greek artists were travelling from their homes, alarmed or threatened by Persian aggression. They disseminated the distinctive style of their work in different media through the rest of the Greek world. In Athens we see their hands and influence in sculpture, architecture and perhaps pottery. In the rich barbarian markets of Etruria, already long conditioned to Greek art by imported works and the proximity of Greek colonial workshops, they found ready employment, and their influence there determined the form of Archaic Etruscan art. The gem-engravers among them founded workshops which may for long have been staffed by Greeks, but which in the fifth and fourth centuries BC produced the wholly distinctive works of Etruscan gem-engraving that retain the old scarab form long after it had been virtually abandoned in the Greek world.

In one of the earliest of these Greek workshops in Etruria, in the years around 530 BC, the scarab *no. 1* was engraved. The beetle back shows much of the elaboration of later scarabs in Etruria with detailed legs, neat stippling on the head and little double-v winglets, but the vertical border to the base is not decorated and the spine is raised in the Greek manner. The intaglio device is surrounded by a cable pattern instead of the usual hatching which appears in this position on most Archaic scarabs, and this is another feature adopted occasionally by gem-engravers in Etruria. The device is purely Greek in style and execution. A youth is shown in the Archaic knee-running pose, holding a jug and kantharos-cup. He is naked and the broad swelling forms of his limbs and body resemble the figures on mid-sixth-century vases. But there is a fullness here too, almost a fleshiness which we associate with East Greek work, and the hair is dressed in exactly the manner of the stone figures of youths found in East Greece, in the Ionian states of Samos and Miletos. This distinctive East Greek coiffure is seen also on other objects in Etruria – notably the colourful water-jars, the 'Caeretan hydriae', made by an immigrant East Greek artist in the Etruscan city of Caere (Cerveteri) for the local market. This vase-painter's career is very like that of our gem-engravers, but unlike them he had no followers.

From about 500 BC, the gem-workshops of Etruria turned to a style which was immediately dependent on that of the Late Archaic Greek artists. It went beyond them in the hard, almost mechanical, treatment of the anatomical studies, in elaboration of the beetle backs, and in the growing habit of polishing the whole surface of the stone. To fit the oval field, Greek engravers had preferred figures in the kneeling-running position, as on *no. 1*. Now, stooping figures are more often found, usually with one leg flexed, or kneeling figures, as well as some groups involving several, a crowding of the field which engravers in Greece generally avoided. The youths on Etruscan gems of the fifth century BC are busy with weapons or athletic equipment, sometimes plying a craft. The popularity of Greek myths encouraged the artists to label the figures with heroic names, inscribed in the Etruscan form, but in the Greek letters which the Etruscans had long before learnt. The youth stooping to pick up a jar on *no. 2* is labelled ΚΑΣΤΥΡ = Kastor. The motif is repeated on a near-contemporary gem which has no inscription. We are not obliged to believe that the artist had in mind any specific act involving the demi-god Kastor. Nor are the other young warriors or athletes on these gems necessarily a Peleus or Tydeus, rather than stock figures enhanced by heroic labels. For that matter, the inscription need not even rule out the possibility that the artist was a Greek; but if so he is working in a style which had by this time been abandoned in the homeland studios. Those who think that our figure must be Kastor engaged in some meaningful activity have to imagine that he is collecting the ashes of his brother Polydeukes (Pollux) in an urn, but in the story it was Kastor who was killed first and Pollux who begged to be allowed to join him. The two-coloured onyx of this stone makes it difficult to view the whole device in original (except through the aid of a variously exposed photographic print). The beetle is finely cut with a tongue pattern on the vertical border, which is regularly decorated on the finer Etruscan seals, a stippled head, but no winglets.

In the Greek world in the fifth century BC, the scarab shape lost its popularity in favour of the 'scaraboid', which was also oval but had its back simply blocked out and lightly domed. The Greek stones were generally now also larger, but *no. 3* is a midget only a quarter of an inch long. On the convex back, there is a hatched border and around the device, instead of the hatched frame, there is a row of pellets, another favourite border in Etruria. This is probably another example of Greek work in the West. The motif is a girl-cock with spread wings. We could call her a siren, were it not for the way that the bird-body is definitely identified as a cock's by the high curving tail-feathers. Ordinary sirens are decidedly female in their iconography and habits, and this must certainly, I think, be taken for a girl's head. But there are a few other girls with cock-bodies in Archaic Greek art – on Athenian vases and on coins, and since there are other cock-monsters on vases and gems, we are probably not obliged to consider this creature a real siren. In the fourth century there are real sirens with cock-bodies which have still to be explained.

After the scaraboid the next development in the shape of gemstones in the Greek world was the ringstone, designed to be set immobile in a metal finger-ring, and not on a swivel or as a pendant. The ringstones only become at all common after the fourth century, but there are a few earlier examples, like *no. 4*, which belongs to shortly before the middle of the fifth century. Both its size and the convex surface on which the device is cut – unlike the flat base of a scarab – are typical of ringstone forms. The gem shows Eros flying, with lyre and wreath, a popular subject on gems and finger-rings of the first half of the fifth century. The slim lines of the young god betoken the new Classical approach to the figure, in contrast with the broad Archaic treatment of figures like that on *no. 1*.

As the Etruscan schools of gem-engraving developed they eschewed the new Greek ringstones and scaraboids, preferring the old scarab form. In their work, two main trends can be observed. One fashion stems immediately from the Late Archaic, with only the slightest concessions to new, Classical modes of representing the human figure, and this 'archaizing' style survives for as long as seals are cut in Etruria. We have two examples, *nos 5* and *6*.

In the athletic scenes on Late Archaic Greek vases, a small boy is often seen carrying his master's kit. The squatting, waiting slave is chosen as a separate motif for gems in the fifth century – for one Greek and two Etruscan, one of which is our *no. 5*. The lad is a negro. From his arm hang his master's oil bottle and strigil. These grotesque squatting poses are especially common for immature or subhuman figures, but they also serve to display virtuosity in representing foreshortened legs.

The beetle of *no. 5* is comparatively simple. On *no. 6* it may lack winglets, but in their place are tiny scrolls such as occasionally appear on other Etruscan gems of this period. A nameless charioteer urges on two horses with a branch-goad. Undisguised use of the drill can be seen in the blob hoofs and joints.

The second trend in Etruscan gem-engraving is a highly decorative one, involving free use of the round-ended drill to block out figures and often a comparatively summary treatment of detail. An inkling of the style appears on *no.7*, which has a finely detailed beetle. In the device the lion-head spout at which the winged goddess fills her jar is barely sketched, while the globular treatment of the goddess's head and her jar betray the new exploitation of technique. By contrast, the feathering of the wings and the drapery folds are carefully shown. In terms of Greek myth this could be Iris filling her golden jar at the waters of the Styx, since it was

16

with this water that the gods swore their most binding oaths [Hesiod, *Theogony* 785]. This is not, however, an event or episode of any importance in Greek iconography, while in Etruria both winged figures and fountain scenes are very popular, so perhaps no identification should be attempted. This may still be fifth-century work and Archaic in conception, but by the end of the century the full effect of the new style, *a globolo*, as it is called, can be seen. A good example is *no. 8*, on which the beetle is carefully cut but with shallow, angular, lifeless detail. The swelling forms of the warrior's helmeted head, buttocks, muscles and shield contrast with the fine linear detail of cuirass and crest, and the sketchy arms and feet. On many *a globolo* gems of the fourth century even this degree of detail is abandoned and the whole figures may be rendered in blobs.

In the third and second centuries BC the history of Italy is told in terms of the rise of Rome. She had shared the culture of Etruria in her earlier days, and her growing power wrought no sudden revolution in the arts. In the gems engraved in Italy we see some influence of the contemporary Hellenistic styles of the Greeks, but in the main it is the older Graeco-Etruscan tradition which is the dominant one. The scarab form is not forgotten, although the beetle has lost all delicacy in its modelling. On *no. 9* there is a good study of an exhausted warrior, in the developed Classical manner. His helmet is that version of the Greek Corinthian helmet which we see on Roman coins from the third century on. The chariot group on *no. 10* is of a type that had a long and distinguished history on coins and in sculpture since the fifth century BC. In this form, with the fan-like splaying of the horses' forelegs and necks, we see the most stylized version which appears on coins by the end of the third century. It is on coins of this date that we see Victory driving the team and holding just such a goad.

More common now are ringstones, set immobile in a metal hoop, like the earlier Greek example *no. 4*. But these Italic ringstones do not much resemble their Greek counterparts. Some retain the Archaic hatched borders of the scarabs and still have flat or barely convex engraved faces, as *nos 11* and *12*. The oval outline may become more angular, as on *no. 11*. This offers a fine study of a stag, and a popular one, to judge from similar gemstones of this date. A cameo in the Ionides Collection [*no. 118*] repeats the motif, but is possibly not ancient. The type goes back to the finer animal studies on Greek gems of the later fifth century and had been treated earlier still in different styles. On *no. 12*, however, there is a wholly indigenous subject. The ritual crook or *lituus* which the old man holds shows that he is an Etruscan seer. His dress and posture are not readily explained. The arts of these men, and their ritual wand, were adopted by the Roman college of Augurs, whose

17

duty it was to foretell events by observation of natural phenomena – the way sacred fowl were feeding and similar occurrences. The Etruscans seem to have been even more obsessed by omens than were the Romans.

With *no. 13* we meet a different shape of gem, an elongated oval, set in its original golden ring. This is a most popular variety and one in which the bezel is very often made of glass, banded black and white to imitate onyx. Here is a particularly fine example, and the young warrior on it is a companion to the older man on *no. 9* – notice their helmets. Looking at these two gems [and *no. 8*] in photographs of the original stones we are forcibly reminded that they were cut to be viewed in impression, which would bring the shield on to the correct, left arm, and the weapons into the right hands.

While these small stones were being cut in Italy, gem-engravers in the Greek world were practising their craft on larger stones and in a style which reflects the new spirit of the Hellenistic Age. The main period of popularity for the scaraboid has passed. The larger oval ringstones approximate to it in shape, although it is the convex surface which is now engraved. Some circular ringstones were also cut, especially in the earlier period, as our *no. 15*. Alexander's conquests in the East had brought within reach a greater variety of semiprecious stones for the Greek studios, and there is a growing interest in the translucent quality of these coloured gems, often now cut and set so that they can best be viewed with the light shining or reflected through them. This is why photographs of the originals of such stones may be as faithful to the artist's conception of his work as photographs of impressions.

It has not always proved easy to distinguish the finer works of the Greek Hellenistic world from their immediate successors of the first century BC which were made in Italy or for Romans. This is not surprising since the latter are made by the same artists as had been working in the Greek east, as we shall see. Some gems can certainly be attributed to the Greek world of the third and second centuries BC for their style and technique, notably the rather soft treatment of exaggeratedly slim figures like those we see in later Hellenistic sculpture and on the gem *no. 14*. Some studies of deities are still very much in the Classical tradition, as *no. 15*, but the borderline between these and the heavily classicizing works of the first century is hard to define. If anything the later works are more mannered, more precise; contrast, for instance, the treatment of the Augustus on *no. 19*. Where portraits of Hellenistic rulers appear, we have a better criterion since these were not generally copied later in the way that many mythological and divine figures certainly were. For these the criteria are yet more difficult, and it is mainly the rougher,

1

17

18

45

almost impressionistic treatment of *no. 16* which suggests that it belongs here rather than in the next chapter.

The Apollo of *no. 14* is a fine example of the pure Hellenistic style, the rather elongated features and limbs, the body softly modelled, and with the distinctively summary treatment of 'props' like the branch and the tripod. This pose, for Apollos, Aphrodites or others, is commonplace on Hellenistic gems, sometimes so mannered as to seem almost a parody.

The strong head on *no. 15* is almost purely fourth-century in type, but was probably cut within the following hundred years. It closely resembles the head of Poseidon on coins of the Macedonian king Antigonos Doson (ruled 229–221 BC), and we may plausibly recognize the same deity here. His is a stormier character than Zeus', and this is often subtly shown in representations of the god – here by the rougher hair and, perhaps, by the parted lips with the teeth just showing. Nineteenth-century collectors sometimes had Greek letters added to their gems to enhance their antiquarian appeal, but the ΥΠ on this gem are probably genuine. If so, they could be the initial letters of either the owner's or the artist's name. Otherwise, we think of the epithet ὕπατος, 'highest', as applied to Zeus, who might alternatively be represented here.

In the sympathetic portrait of an elderly woman on *no. 17*, Furtwängler thought he saw the Greek queen of Egypt, Arsinoe II, towards the end of her life (she died in 270 BC, aged about 46). The many portraits of her on coins show her younger and are more flattering. The type is invariable for these Ptolemaic queens, with a veil drawn over the head, but we miss the fillet or diadem usually shown also just below the veil. Their necks are rather fleshy and wrinkled – variously explained in terms of the admired 'Venus rings' or as a goitrous condition which ran in the family. Here a double chin intervenes. Furtwängler's identification seems not to have won approval or to have been ignored by students of Ptolemaic iconography. If the gem does not show Arsinoe, it can at least be confidently taken for a portrait of an Alexandrian Greek lady of the Ptolemaic court, and perhaps of the royal family.

To judge from the confident and bold cutting of the scene on *no. 16* this is another Hellenistic gem. Later treatment of this subject would have rendered the anatomy, features and tree in greater detail but with less sculptural force. The old satyr has hung up his pipes and sits tired and somewhat fuddled in a pose long employed in Greek art for similar, although generally heroic subjects – the bemused mad Ajax, sulking Achilles, even the sad, patient Penelope. Here the comparative triviality of the subject takes nothing from the dignity of the figure. We might recognize here Marsyas, defeated by Apollo, who has hung his now useless pipes on the tree to which he will soon be bound, to be flayed for his presumption. Such representations are seen on gems but it should be the reed pipes (*auloi*) that he played, and not the bagpipes, as here. However, the Marsyas scenes probably inspired this picture.

CHAPTER III

Roman Gems

'The first man to own a considerable number of gems in Rome (we use the foreign term "dactyliotheca" – "cabinet of rings") was Sulla's stepson Scaurus. For a long time there was no other until Pompey the Great included King Mithridates' cabinet with other dedications on the Capitol. Varro and other authorities of that time declare it inferior to Scaurus'. Caesar, during his dictatorship, followed this example by dedicating six cabinets in the Temple of Venus Genetrix, and Marcellus, Octavian's son, dedicated one in the Temple of Apollo on the Palatine. But it was Pompey's victory over Mithridates that promoted the fashion for pearls and gemstones' [Pliny, *Natural History* iv 11–12].

By the establishment of the Roman province of Achaea the Greek homeland had been compassed by Rome by the middle of the second century BC. Soon afterwards, the Hellenistic kingdom of Pergamum was bequeathed to Rome by Attalus III to form the core of the new province of Asia, and Romans had already interfered in the affairs of the Ptolemies in Egypt. Pompey's victories, which led to the formation of the new province of Syria, were the culmination of a century of military and political activity which gave the Hellenistic world of Greece and the Near East to Rome. At the same time, Hellenistic Greek art and artists became better known in Italy, offering fresher inspiration than could be won from the arts of the Greek colonies in the West. In gem-engraving the new Hellenistic styles were already being copied, although on a minor scale, as we have seen. It took a new influx from the courts of the Hellenistic kings to promote the collecting of

23

engraved gems in Roman society and to inaugurate the great new period of engraving by Greek artists for Roman patrons in Italy and other parts of the Roman world. This new influence was to determine the classicizing aspect of early Roman art in much the way that the influence of East Greek artists five hundred years before had determined the course of Etruscan art.

The first century BC is the period of Antony, Caesar and Octavian, who became Augustus, first Emperor in Rome; when the Republic was forged into an Empire; when Roman art was at its most Hellenized, despite the very different interests and temperament of those who commissioned the works. In some ways it repeats the story of Greek influence in Etruria in earlier years, and again it can be as well illustrated in the art of the gem-engraver as in any other art. It is an important period, moreover, because it was the one best appreciated in later centuries, and the art of the Late Republic and Early Empire remained a model of perfection for the Roman world. In its most classic form it was the style most admired by the Renaissance and so a vital connecting link in the history of Western art.

The style, as we judge it on the gemstones, is not so much that of the monumental sculpture of the day, although there is much in common with the so-called 'neo-Attic' reliefs, but of the miscalled 'minor' arts. Coins, for their size and subject matter, provide a ready comparison, but the dies from which they were struck were rarely of the high quality of many gems, and since coins were mass-produced we are familiar with almost all the types, while each gemstone is a unique document and every new discovery enriches our knowledge. Nevertheless, the die-cutters were surely found among gem-engravers. Closer to the gems, and especially to the impressions taken from them, are various classes of clay relief. The most informative of these are the so-called Campana reliefs, which are decorative plaques serving as wall revetments, and the Arretine bowls. The earliest of the reliefs and bowls are close contemporaries of the best Early Roman gems, comparable in style and often subject. Although the art of the gem-engraver is an independent and distinguished one, it cannot be studied without reference to these cognate works by the coroplast and potter. For its subject matter the whole range of Roman art has to be considered – the works of painter, mosaicist and sculptor.

The shapes of the gems cut in Rome or for Romans do not differ much from those of the Hellenistic Greek world. Circular stones are perhaps less common and oval ones rather broader. Size is not appreciably increased; indeed, on average they are smaller, except for pieces designed for pendants, and most were easily set in finger-rings or small ornaments. Materials too differed little from the Hellenistic, with a great variety of coloured translucent stones coming from the East and Egypt.

The identification of some of these without proper apparatus (especially a refracto-meter) can be difficult, but there are some easily recognized stones. Garnets are especially popular, notably the richly coloured almandine for finer works. These are often chosen to be cut on a heavily domed surface, as on a natural pebble (*en cabochon*), and with the back hollowed out so that the thickness of the stone is even. The term 'carbuncle' is regularly used of these. A great range of palest red and yellow translucent stones is employed – pale cornelian, topaz, jacinth. In the best period amethyst is preferred for the finer stones, sometimes an almost clear quartz with amethystine patches. The rarer emerald or sapphire is seldom encountered. Apart from the carbuncles, smaller stones may be cut with a high convex face but a flat back, bevelled at the edges for setting, which allows very high relief in the cutting and favours frontal or three-quarter views of heads. This is another fashion derived from earlier Greek usage. The gems with a more shallow convex face also usually have a flat polished back, rarely lightly convex or concave, but some small stones have a very heavily domed back. These were certainly mounted in open bezels although many of the others, as we have already observed [above, *p. 11*], were backed with gold or silver foil which reflected the light through the stone. The bevelling of the edges at the back is rarely pronounced. A shape only met commonly after the best period has a heavily bevelled edge to the flat engraved face, rather like a truncated cone. This is necessary when the stone used is banded in parallel strata, like an onyx or nicolo, and a flat face is needed for the engraving which may (as usually on nicolo) be cut through to a different colour, rather like a reverse cameo.

In the Hellenistic and Early Roman period, copies of engraved gems were often made of glass, usually called 'paste', which had been cast in baked clay impressions taken from the original stones. Occasionally they are coloured to imitate plain or banded stones and sometimes not cast with the intaglio but individually engraved. Some 'pastes' are our only evidence for the existence of types not represented on extant stones.

The practice of cutting gemstones in relief began in the Greek world with the Archaic pseudo-scarabs on which the beetle back is replaced by a head or figure cut in high relief or half-round. Other minor ornaments were cut in a similar manner but only one scarab back seems also to exploit the colour differences of banded stone. Not until the Hellenistic period does the normal 'cameo' type appear, to be set then in a finger-ring or pendant. Banded chalcedonies are chosen – agate or sardonyx – and these are readily imitated in glass. The pattern is cut in the pale layer with the underlying dark layer serving as the background. By cutting the pale layer thin, a translucent effect can be achieved. Occasionally two or even three (exceptionally four) layers are cut in relief over the background, giving a greater range of colour effects. For these the banded stones have to be most carefully cut, but simpler cameos can be very easily prepared by using the pale altered surface of a natural pebble for the relief, with the dark core as the background. Ordinary flint pebbles, such as we find in England, present white surfaces over a dark core, and flint is a hydrated silica, like chalcedony. The discolouration or patina is explained as the 'drying out' of the surface which becomes both paler and softer. When a pebble is broken, the break itself in time clouds over in the same way. The effect on stones of the chalcedony family accounts for most of those gems described as of 'burnt cornelian' or the like, and thought to have been discoloured in the funeral pyre. This is more likely the result of the conditions of burial or exposure to the air in a built tomb. Where the paler colour goes right through the stone it may have been simply an opaque pale chalcedony or mottled. Stones used for gems do not neatly obey the rules of identity we lay down for the differently named variants. Many names we use for the stones simply describe colour variations in a single family, but in antiquity the colour may have been more important than the composition. Thus, to the chalcedonies belong cornelian (red); sard (brown); agate (in its varieties, banded or moss-agate); onyx (white-and-black straight layers); sardonyx (white and brown); bloodstone or heliotrope (green speckled red); chrysoprase (apple green); plasma (bright green); and closely related are the various coloured opaque jaspers. In antiquity there was a further distinction of sex for some stones, the male being dark and opaque, the female pale and transparent. Many terms in use today by students of gems or dealers are not recognized by geologists. Much of the terminology is a matter of convenience; some of it, one suspects, obscurantism. The descriptions given below are true to the appearance of the stones if not always to their composition. 'But there is no end to the names given to precious stones, and I have no intention of listing them in full, innumerable as they are, thanks to the wanton imagination of the Greeks.' Pliny may have the last word [*Natural History* xxxvii 75].

The subjects chosen for engraving are readily classified. Portraits of notables, generals and emperors, continue a fashion set by the Hellenistic royal families and, like them, assimilation to a deity if not actual deification may be alluded to by adding divine attributes. Heads and figures of divinities are common, especially those most favoured by the Romans or appropriate as signet devices, like Fortuna. Some deities and mythological scenes are popular because they recall the foundation stories of Rome, like those showing Aeneas or Venus, or because noble families

26

claimed descent from a like source. The *gens Julia*, of Caesar and Augustus, counted Aeneas and Venus in their ancestry, and this may account for much of the popularity of gems showing Venus or Erotes, although these would have a natural appeal also. Antony saw himself as a young Dionysos, and his intimate dealings with the Hellenistic courts of the Greek world ensured a patronage for gem-engraving and continued popularity for Dionysiac subjects. The degree of symbolism involved in the choice of subjects or subsidiary devices is less easily judged on gems than it is on coins, but it is clearly an important factor. Compositions are clear, simple and not usually cluttered by superfluous effects. They fill the field easily and completely. All these principles had been observed in earlier Greek work to an even higher degree, and ignorance of them betrays the copyist.

The intaglio gems of the Ionides Collection mostly belong to the best period, of the first centuries BC and AD, with some more trivial but interesting pieces of later centuries. The most obvious examples of the latter are grouped at the end [*nos 53–5*]. Of the other stones the portraits are considered first, then representations of gods and mythological figures or scenes, and finally animals and monsters. In view of the Greek style and iconography of most of these gems, I keep the Greek names for the deities shown on them, only calling them by their Roman names when their attributes or behaviour identify them more closely with the Roman deity.

The head of Mark Antony on *no. 18* is an important addition to his known portraits and hitherto unpublished. The name of the artist, Gnaios, appears behind the head in the typically neat letters of his signature. Four other gems with Gnaios' signature are surely authentic. His style has been studied by Miss Vollenweider and well characterized for its soft contours and broad polished surfaces, especially in portraits. Antony died in 41 BC, and the portraits of the last years of his life show him thus, clean shaven. These are the years he spent in the East, after Philippi, and even if his coins are more brutally realistic, we might expect a Greek artist, in the court of Alexandria, to Hellenize and idealize his features in this way – but by no means beyond recognition. Another explanation for this rather flattering portrait might be that it was cut after his death. Miss Vollenweider has shown reason to believe that Gnaios moved to work in Numidia (approximately modern Algeria) at the court of Juba II. The king had married Cleopatra Selene, a daughter of Antony and Cleopatra, and he was himself an expert on precious stones, several times cited by Pliny. There would be nothing strange in the artist remaining in the employment of the family, and in his superb portrait of a queen, now in New York, it may not be too fanciful to see the head of Cleopatra Selene herself.

The artist's name, Gnaios, is a Roman *praenomen*, Gnaeus. The same is true of Aulos, another gem-engraver, who declares himself son of Alexas, a Greek. There is therefore no reason to believe that Gnaios was not Greek. In the Ptolemaic period another Roman *praenomen*, Gaios, is to be found in the Greek world, and especially at Alexandria, carried by Greeks. Even in the early second century BC an Athenian priest bore the name.

The Augustus from the Marlborough Collection, *no. 19*, has been attributed by Miss Vollenweider to the master Solon. Hermes/Mercury's caduceus in the field characterizes the Emperor as the New Mercury. In the second poem of his first book of Odes, written in 28 BC, the Roman poet Horace looks to the young Augustus, his last opponent defeated, to set Rome to rights. 'What god shall the people call to succour the collapsing state?' An Apollo, Venus or Mars, – 'or if, with changed form, you take the disguise of a youth, winged son of gentle Maia, and agree to be hailed avenger of Caesar'. Other texts and monuments attest Augustus' equation with Hermes, the 'winged son of gentle Maia'. It is this divine identity which has idealized the portrait on our gem to a degree not admitted on contemporary coins. The stone is broken and would have been a full oval some six centimetres high, giving the figure to just above the waist. Another Marlborough gem, now in the British Museum, is its companion piece in style, stone and size. It shows Augustus' sister Octavia, characterized as Diana by a hunting spear set upright before her in the same position as the caduceus. She faces right (on the stone), her brother left. It is tempting to assume that they were set together in some way to form an antithetic pair. If so, it is hard to imagine them set as free hanging pendants, which is the likely explanation of many such large intaglios of this period. They were surely set in such a way that the translucent quality of the thin cut stone could be appreciated, probably with a polished gold backing. The light banding of the agate enhances the otherworldly aspect of the imperial figures. The other Roman intaglios illustrated here are all of a size appropriate to setting in finger-rings and could be used as signets. Although signet-usage determined the form of the two Marlborough gems, it is unlikely that they were used for sealing.

On *no. 20* Augustus wears the radiate crown of a deity, so the gem was cut after his death (in AD 14) and deification. The type of crown with the thin rays standing vertically on the fillet derives from that worn by the Ptolemies. Augustus appears thus on coins struck under his successor Tiberius, on which he is named *Divus Augustus Pater*.

Deities shown full-figure on gems can usually be recognized by their attributes. With heads alone the classicizing features and beards distinguish the divine from the mortal in some periods, but goddesses may go unidentified, and the assimilation of an emperor or general to a divinity, as we have seen with Augustus, provides another possible source of error.

Figures of Zeus/Jupiter enthroned, as on *no. 21*, are generally taken for copies of Pheidias' famous cult statue at Olympia, which held a figure of Victory in its outstretched hand and an eagle atop its sceptre. The statue was often copied for the cult statues in other temples, and when shown with different attributes on coins or gems, as here, some other version could be intended. One obvious model might be the statue of Jupiter Capitolinus, installed in Rome after Sulla's death, but it seems that only its first-century AD replacement sat on a high-backed throne like that shown on the gem. Here the god's eagle is on the ground, he holds a sceptre and patera (?), and there may be a Victory perched on the throne back.

The Jupiter of *no. 22* wears the ram's horns of the Egyptian god Amun. As Zeus Ammon he had been worshipped in Egypt at Siwa Oasis where there was an oracle much respected by the Greeks. Alexander's visit to the sanctuary and identification with the deity, illustrated by his portraits on which he too wears the horns, renewed the popularity of the cult. This type, with the three-quarter head, becomes very popular on gems from the Hellenistic period on.

Another of the more popular deities introduced to the Greek world from Egypt in the Hellenistic period was Sarapis, assimilated to Zeus/Jupiter. He is shown wearing the *modius*, a basket-shaped headdress, on *nos 23* and *24*. On the latter his shaggy, spindly locks recall the 'Zeus Otricoli'-type in sculpture, which is often seen also for the head of the seated cult statue, as that on our *no. 21*. Yet another type, *no. 25*, shows the sculptured bust of the god as it would appear at the top of a pillar or herm [compare *no. 87*]. Hermes' head belongs on such pillars in Greece, but it became a common base for portraits of philosophers and statesmen. This use for other deities is less often met, but just such a 'Jupiter Terminalis' is seen on coins of the first century BC.

On run-of-the-mill ringstones the heads or figures of certain deities seem especially popular. The goddess Fortuna is one, and *no. 26* is a comparatively well-cut example of the subject. Her stance is that of a Hellenistic goddess, small-breasted, heavy-hipped. The steering oar she holds in one hand betokens her control of man's destiny; the cornucopia and branches, her bestowal of bounty.

A symptom of Roman obsession with foreign deities is Pantheism. Some coins of Mark Antony show a mixed deity, and with the early Empire we find more reference to and representation of *panthea signa*. On *no. 27a* a figure of Apolline type is given an Egyptian crown. The other side of the gem, *no. 27b*, is cut as a

29

cameo with a more involved hybrid deity. The attributes of the Sun (rays), Isis (crown), Mercury (winged heels), Jupiter (thunderbolt) and Fortuna (cornucopia) are worn or carried by a childlike figure, probably Horus. This combination of cameo and intaglio is odd, and the stone could only have effectively been worn as a pendant. For its style the intaglio is far poorer than the cameo, and it was probably added by another artist.

In studies of gods other than these formal portraits we commonly see them with some divine transport. Figures riding hippocamps become a popular motif in the first century BC. Nereids or other marine deities, even Eros, are usually the passengers; compare the creature carrying Poseidon on *no. 82*. On *no. 28* the lady carries a thyrsos and so should be a maenad. The thyrsos is not commonly seen in the hands of anyone outside Dionysos' band, but can on occasion be picked up by a centaur, even a Victory, in Roman art. Dionysos was a sea-goer both in cult and in his encounter with the pirates, in which he turned them into dolphins. A dolphin helps support our 'maenad'. When Eros rides a dolphin he is copying heroic figures like Arion, Taras or Palaimon. With his trident on the gold ring, *no. 29*, he is not so much stealing Poseidon's attribute as doing some idle fishing. He is seen on dolphins on Roman coins of about 74 BC and on many Roman sarcophagi. Normally, he carries a whip, although a gem, a fragmentary Campana relief and a later mosaic show him with a trident, as here. Solid gold rings with the intaglio cut in the metal had been popular since the fifth century BC in Greece, but here the decorated field is clearly imitating the setting of an engraved gemstone and the older type of ring, with the large bezel fitted to a simple hoop, has been forgotten.

No. 30 offers a rather crude rendering of a popular version of Heracles, grizzled, and weary from his labours.

Mark Antony identified himself as a New Dionysos, but this could have done no more than contribute to the continued popularity of Dionysiac themes in early Roman art. The god of wine, conviviality and mysteries, could never fall from favour, and the behaviour of his troop entertained by reflecting the more carnal aspirations of mortals. The drunken satyr or young Dionysos staggering forward with raised and sadly empty wine jug was a much-loved motif in the last century BC and much copied in later times, as our *no. 94*. Finer specimens, known from ancient 'paste' (glass) copies in Berlin excited Winckelmann's admiration and ensured its currency in eighteenth-century classicizing art. Beside the study of the young god on *no. 31* we have a signature giving the first three letters, followed by a dot, of the name of the artist Hyllos, son of the great engraver Dioskourides. Although the name was taken in vain by late copyists the style of the letters and the rare abbreviation, along with the confident clear style of the intaglio, declare for the authenticity of this piece, which can be added to the gems signed by or attributed to Hyllos. To judge from the number of these gems surviving he was a prolific artist. While the specimen shown here is far from being his finest work, it has a confident strength and is of some interest for its subject. Hyllos' *floruit* was around 20 BC.

In head studies Dionysos is given youthful, effeminate features, and massive wreathes of vines and ivy which would do credit to Ascot. Such heads are commonly seen on sarcophagi and clay reliefs. We have here two examples on gems: *no. 32*, rare for its material and shape, a diamond-shaped emerald, and *no. 33*, a more prosaic, deep-cut garnet. In Dionysos' entourage satyrs may be of any age. An elderly one is seen drinking from a cup on *no. 34*, in a pose clearly related to the Marsyas-type of *no. 17*, and possibly still late Hellenistic in date. On *no. 35* there is the wreathed bust of a similar figure.

Pan was a deity in his own right to the Greeks. His goat-like character, appearance and behaviour made him an honorary member of Dionysos' band, a companion of satyrs. In Rome he was identified with the rustic deity, Faunus. It is as a Greek, and for his association with Dionysos, but as a god of the theatre, that he is shown on *no. 36* shouldering a thyrsos and studying a stage mask. More specifically stage or theatrical themes are common on gems. The actor on *no. 37*, cloaked and leaning on a crook, is a familiar figure. This is an uncommonly sympathetic portrayal of a paunchy, reflective Pagliaccio, and the tragic mask on the pillar beside him may be set there in a deliberately symbolic contrast with the comic mask he is wearing. A close copy of the whole scene appears on a cameo in Vienna. The seated comic on *no. 38* is a poorer but entertaining study. Masks, as *nos 39* and *40*, become commonplace decorative motifs.

Other mythological subjects also derive almost wholly from the repertory of Greek Hellenistic art. The head of the Gorgon Medusa, who turns man to stone by her glance, was shown by Archaic Greek artists as a grinning, menacing lion-mask with human ears and snake locks. In the Classical period, her looks are sweetened until she is shown as a lovely girl, more deadly than the male, more effectively so for her beauty tempered only by the snakes knotted neatly beneath her chin, and the wings in her wild hair. We show two late versions. The Hellenistic example on *no. 41* has a full-fleshy face, unkempt hair but skimpy snakes. The type of the famous Medusa Rondanini, whose origin lies in the high Classical period, is represented by a fine cameo copy of late Renaissance date, *no. 98*, and a poorer Roman cameo, with the deadly glance averted, *no. 73*.

The Medusa head is seen again on *no. 42*, but as centrepiece to the device of the

31

triskeles, with three ears of corn. This refers to Sicily, which had long used the three legs as its blazon, and had been an important source of grain for both Greece and Rome. The device had appeared on some Hellenistic coins, as of Panormus (Palermo), and in this form it also appears on coins of 49 BC, issued in Sicily by the consuls Lentulus and Marcellus. Whether this alone was enough to ensure its renewed popularity is far from clear, but it becomes a common motif on gems. What is seriously wrong on our stone is that one leg is going in the wrong direction, which a Sicilian would probably have judged a poor-enough joke.

The subject of *no. 43*, the long-tressed nymph with the gleaming shoulders, is seen on several gems and is generally taken for a swimming Nereid or Amphitrite, but other notable swimmers have been proposed of either sex, like Leander or Leucothea. Galene, the personification of the calm sea, is a favourite candidate. An epigram in the Palatine Anthology [ix 544] describes a beryl engraved with a representation of her by the artist Tryphon in the mid first century BC:

> Tryphon persuaded me, an Indian beryl, to be Galene and with his gentle hands let down my hair. Look at my lips, smoothing the liquid sea, and my breasts with which I beguile the calm. Did but the jealous stone consent you would soon see me really swimming, as I long to.

It is improbable, however, that the device on Tryphon's gem was anything like our *no. 43*, since the girl's lips are not much in evidence and her breasts not at all. The type appears on coins of about 70 BC, but must be Hellenistic in origin, and it is even possible that our gem is Hellenistic in date. Although other gems show this subject, ours alone has the crescent added, which could be a clue to identity. The name which comes first to mind is Selene, goddess of the moon, regularly shown in Greek art as a head or bust, taken to be emerging from or entering the waves. A frontal bust of her with the crescent shown beside her head appears on a phalera of the early first century BC. Even if the type did not signify Selene from the first, our artist may well have intended her to be identified on this gem. Figures like this, seen in a three-quarter back view and showing a cold shoulder, are met often on Arretine bowls, and the motif is Hellenistic in origin.

Myths relating to Rome's past were naturally much approved. Scenes of Rome's hero-founder, Aeneas, rescuing his father and family from burning Troy, had been singled out in sixth-century Athens for vases destined for Italy. As mentioned, the *gens Julia* claimed relationship to Aeneas and through him to his mother Venus. Soon Virgil's epic was to ensure the continued popularity of the theme. The Aeneas and Anchises group is seen on Roman coins of 48 BC. The gems, as our *no. 44*, add the child Ascanius or Julus, wearing his Phrygian cap (compare his countryman

Ganymede on *no. 45*) and shouldering his throwing stick. There was a closely similar gem with this scene in the Evans Collection, which also has this strange way of showing the shaggy surface of Aeneas' cloak, falling below Anchises. It omits the cicada or other insect which is put between Aeneas' legs on our stone. The significance of this is not clear, but it may be the symbol of a particular family, and we may note the popularity of the cicada as a subsidiary device on Roman coins of the 80's BC.

The fine 'carbuncle', *no. 45*, presents another Trojan scene. Ganymede offering the eagle a drink is usually shown either stroking the eagle's head or caressing its neck, but this version, with the boy resting one hand on his rocky seat, is also to be found. He was carried up to Olympus to serve as wine boy for the gods and Zeus' favourite, and it is generally thought that these scenes show him serving Zeus' eagle with water as he did the gods with wine. On early scenes of the rape (or rather seduction) Zeus himself carried off the boy, and this makes it probable that in the normal later version of the story, where he is borne aloft by an eagle, this is Zeus in one of the many animal-disguises he assumed for amorous purposes. If so, there was no reason for him to remain an eagle on Olympus, to be watered by Ganymede. And is this Olympus? The rocks and tree are terrestrial enough, and the tree is often shown in these scenes. Ganymede is wearing his Phrygian cap, appropriate to a Trojan prince, but discarded in scenes which obviously show him in Olympus. Moreover, on a bronze coin of Troy this scene has a Trojan setting with Athena's image set on a column in the background. In a Pompeii wall-painting, Eros is leading the eagle to Ganymede, and on a Roman sarcophagus and other objects he is also in attendance. Was there a version of the story in which the Zeus-eagle wins Ganymede's confidence by feigning exhaustion and being given sustenance, or perhaps simply by being a handsome, friendly bird? On our gem Ganymede looks apprehensive enough: on the other versions he shows how he is attracted to the creature, which he caresses, and when he is carried aloft, he goes quietly. This would have been a typical confidence trick on the part of the father of the gods. Nemesis-Leda received the Zeus-swan because it appeared to be flying terrified from Zeus' eagle: a closely comparable situation.

Troy again, and the Greek hero Diomedes' rape of the Palladion – the cult-image of Athena. The scene of his escape was much favoured by first-century BC gem-engravers, and fine versions signed by Felix, Gnaios, Solon and Dioskourides have survived, as well as many copies. The version on *no. 46* is a comparatively summary one, with some interesting features. All but Solon had shown the hero climbing across the altar, rather as on our stone, but already holding the image and with another statue on a pillar at hand. Felix's gem, now in Oxford, shows that this happens on his flight from Troy, outside the city's walls and apparently in a sanctuary of Poseidon. However, we see the episode as on our stone on another nicolo, in the Beverley Collection. The hero seems to be actually lifting the image from a pillar, yet escaping over the altar in the same leaping pose. The Beverley gem has also the statue on a pillar seen on other gems, and it looks as though it is confusing the iconography of the theft with that of the get-away. It has also various symbolic additions, like a branch, star, moon and ship's prow. Only the last is copied on our simplified version (beyond the altar), but the type of the Beverley gem is clearly the model for we see the same folds of material beyond the Palladion. A late Roman sarcophagus has Odysseus present, as he is on the Felix gem, but the pillar is bare and could presumably be taken for the one robbed of its statue.

Another simple nicolo, *no. 47*, shows Odysseus, weary from his travels, sitting on a roller (?) outside his home. He is disguised as a beggar. Fuller versions of the scene on gems and on wall-paintings from houses at Pompeii show Penelope approaching him. A later artist or owner of our stone took the roller for a tub and added the name Diogenes to the gem. The roller or drum is unusual enough as furniture and is presumably shown in these scenes as a typical courtyard object which might be used as a casual seat.

On *no. 48* the heavily muscled body of a young man buckles slightly under the weight of a nearly full-grown calf. A version of the group on a gem signed by Anteros in the collection of the Duke of Devonshire seems to characterize the figure as Heracles by the lion-skin on the hero's shoulder beneath the animal's body. This is the group copied on another Ionides gem, *no. 81*, and it is also seen on pastes in Berlin, a four-sided Italic gem in Boston and a cameo in the Beverley Collection. That this is the sequel to Heracles' encounter with the Cretan bull is far from certain, however, since the creature looks very small and its tiny horns and large floppy ears are most like a calf's. On our gems the horns are not shown at all (indeed the head looks more equine), there is a cloak not a lion-skin, and the youth is wreathed like a reveller or a victor in games. The scheme of the group is certainly Heraclean, going back to Archaic scenes of Heracles carrying the Erymanthian boar in just this way. In his mission against the Cretan bull he had also to bring it back alive, so the scheme could easily have been transferred to the other story. Another explanation which has been offered for this type is that the figure is Milo, the famous athlete of the sixth century BC. He had lived at Kroton in Sicily, and the best-known story of his strength told how he carried a four-year-old

34

calf through the stadium at Olympia. He killed and ate it on the same day. A statue was erected for him, but certainly no such group as this, and it is not an event likely to be celebrated thus so late. A further complication is the appearance of the figure exactly as it is shown on the Anteros gem on a Campana clay relief of about the same date. There the calf-carrier is followed by a conventional figure of Winter, carrying a hare, birds and a boar, and the whole scene looks more like preparation for a feast despite the skin on the youth's shoulder. But animal skins may be worn or carried by mortals on rustic occasions, and does this have to be a lion-skin – the lion's head is never shown? Yet another example of the figure, on a glass vase from Kyzikos in London, is also accompanied by figures of the Seasons and the calf-carrier has neither cloak nor animal skin. The Archaic calf-carrier, *moschophoros*, from the Athenian Acropolis could never be mistaken for a Heracles, but is a worshipper bringing an animal for sacrifice and the feast. Possibly we should reconsider the identification of this 'new' type for Heracles and the bull. It is certainly not one admitted to Roman representations of the whole cycle of Heracles' labours.

The other themes on the Roman gems are more trivial. The chubby boy with two cocks on *no. 49* has no wings but is behaving as Eros and should probably be so identified. The creation of a coin or gem device by combining heads or bodies of different animals and human beings, as on *nos 50* and *51*, is of considerable antiquity. Several are seen in the fifth century on Graeco-Phoenician gems, and Achaemenid finger-rings known from impressions found at Ur. On several of these the main head is that of a man whose beard is impersonated by a bird. This is probably the origin of the later type which regularly includes bird's legs and a bearded head, but without the same subtle confusion of parts. The earliest example of the new form appears on a clay mould found recently at Stratos in Acarnania and datable to the early third century BC; this demonstrates that the type best known to us from Roman gems was evolved in Hellenistic Greece. The late monsters are often miscalled *grylloi* – a term best reserved for caricatures or representations of deformed humans. The components and surgery involved are fairly stereotyped, and the hybrids shown here are absolutely standard. *No. 50* also carries a Latin motto invoking victory for a person, perhaps the owner, identified only by his initials. In the style and spirit of these monsters are the many more domestic groups of animal heads in threes or fours, as that on *no. 52*.

Finally, some intaglio heads can be certainly attributed to later Roman periods. The head on *no. 53* presents some difficulties: though intended for an Emperor, he is not readily identified unless this is an unusually idealized portrait of the young

Nero. The signature gives us the name Photios, in the genitive, and the letters Athe... The latter might be the initial letters of the artist's home, Athens, or of his father. In either case an odd usage.

Poor Pescennius Niger was proclaimed Emperor while governor of Syria in AD 193, but he never saw Rome again and was killed by Septimius Severus in the next year. We recognize him on *no. 54* from his portraits on coins, struck for him in the East, and this may have been cut for him or his family during or just after his brief bid for fame.

Gems showing the heads of married couples, as on *no. 55*, become more common in the second century AD. These are private persons and not identified. The way the man dresses his beard and the woman her hair points to the late second century, the period of Marcus Aurelius, and the heads on the coins of Faustina, Lucilla or Crispina.

CHAPTER IV

Roman Cameos

The materials and methods involved in making cameo gems were described in the last chapter [*pp. 25–26*]. Most cameos are no bigger than the intaglio gems but there are some which are considerably larger, and the techniques of cutting semiprecious stones in high relief were applied also to vases and small figures in the round. These bring us closest to the technical skills, although fortunately not the taste, of a modern Fabergé. The range of subjects on cameos is much as that on engraved gems: fewer deities, perhaps, except for those scenes dealing with the affairs of Dionysos or Aphrodite; fewer portraits; repetition of certain other types, like the Victory which is the subject of the first to be discussed here.

The cameo *no. 56* showing Nike-Victory in her chariot (sometimes identified as Eos-Dawn) is the best example in this collection of the use of a layered onyx which permitted a three-colour scheme in the use of the upper dark layer. This is cut for the hair and the drapery at the shoulder of the Victory, her chariot and the near horse, all but its mane which is carved in the second, white layer, together with the other horse, the ground line and the rest of the Victory. The theme is commonplace on cameos; here rendered with especial care.

The large elephant cameo from the Marlborough Collection, *no. 57*, is an important and puzzling piece. The creature is shown trampling on and goring a massive fish, and while this motif suggests various explanations, from the wholly symbolic to the wholly realistic, none seem quite decisive. With so much symbolism attested on early Roman coins and gems, such a strange scene encourages any attempt at interpretation in symbolic terms. The elephant appears on coins as a symbol of the *gens Caecilia*, but of greater possible relevance is its use for Julius Caesar himself. Servius' commentary on Virgil suggests that this was because his forefather had killed one, and the name for elephant in Punic was *'caesar'* or the like. Whatever the reason alleged the connection is explicit enough when, on coins struck in Gaul in the mid first century BC, an elephant is shown trampling upon the traditional Gaulish war trumpet (*carnyx*) which has a massive serpent-head terminal. On the cameo this is no serpent trumpet but a real fish, and it is none too easy to find an explanation for it on these lines. We get nearer to the idea of the struggle of two symbolic animals, and to the composition, on coins showing a bull trampling and goring a wolf, which were minted during the Social War of 91–88 BC by the rebels. Here the Sabellian bull is worrying the wolf of Rome. It might just be possible that a crocodile was intended on the cameo, but the creatures had been seen in Rome already in 58 BC, and no Roman artist would have shown one so fish-like, although the head of the monster corresponds well enough. Moreover, the crocodile did not become for the Romans the symbol of Egypt until some time after Caesar's death.

While it remains tempting to search for a symbolic explanation of the scene, it is still possible to refer it to the accounts of elephants fighting serpent-like creatures which appear in Pliny. For elephants and crocodiles we may recall the Roman mosaics and painted scenes of a crocodile pulling a cow by its muzzle into the Nile. This must have inspired Rudyard Kipling's 'Just-So Story' of How the Elephant's Child got his Trunk, on the banks of the great grey green, greasy Limpopo River.

The gross old silen with his young companion on the cameo *no. 58* give an excellent example of the Dionysiac themes popular on first-century gems. From Miss Vollenweider's study of the signed work of the artist Sostratos, and pieces attributed to his hand, he is shown to be a master of this genre. Our cameo is surely his work too, of the mid first century BC or little after. The use of the drill on hair and features, the sensuous rendering of bodies and limbs are hallmarks of his style.

The tiny figures of *no. 59* do not tell against its antiquity, for there are none of the gratuitous additions of furniture and scenery which characterize eighteenth-century versions. This is one of several rather trivial but engaging works in the manner of the finer cameos of Sostratos. The pillar in the background supports a figure of Priapus, such as often appears in these scenes of sacrifice, and whom a satyr, as the one on the left here, can appropriately serve. He is playing double pipes; not the straight type we see on Greek vases, but the so-called Phrygian pipes which appear on many Roman works, with one pipe straight, the other curved

56   57

58

71

like a horn. There are many versions of this whole scene on Roman gems. A cameo
in Vienna leaves out the pillar with Priapus and the altar, and on other stones
various combinations of piping satyr, woman and altar, the pillar, and the man
with the goat are seen.

The Hellenistic idylls and novelettes of the court at Alexandria popularized stories like that of Eros–Cupid and Psyche, while Roman families who attempted to
trace their lineage back to Venus must have encouraged literal erotic symbolism
in art. Not all the scenes, however, need be fraught with hidden meaning. It may
seem odd that putti should be involved in any so material activity as erecting a
trophy, yet they are thus engaged on *no. 60*. Their victories are bloodless but they
deserve to celebrate them none the less. Erotes are seen erecting trophies on a few
other gems and some are so occupied in a frieze from the Temple of Venus Genetrix in Rome. Sometimes Eros simply shoulders a trophy, and for reverses on the
field of love compare the signed gem by Aulos showing Eros bound to a trophy.
The style of our cameo comes close to that of the cameo signed by the mid-first-
century artist Tryphon, and of a cameo attributed to him by Miss Vollenweider,
showing Erotes again busy with erection – this time trying to lift Heracles' club.
Elsewhere we see them erecting Priapus pillars.

Eros is seen riding animals almost as soon as he is represented at all in Greek
art, but not until the fourth century does he take to horseback. The fine cameo,
no. 61, has him on a high-stepping horse, like a triumphant general. More often he
is shown at full gallop, like the little Paul Revere figures on first-century BC Roman
coins, who may wear cloaks or carry palm branches, and are on rare occasions
shown winged. The set of the figure recalls the fine cameo of Eros riding a lion,
by Protarchos, dated in the early first century. Our cameo may be as early and
could even be his work. To his hand Miss Vollenweider attributes a cameo in
Naples showing Aphrodite and Eros with Hermaphrodite. The figure of Hermaphrodite on *no. 62* is very like this in pose, hair style and drapery, and quite like in
features. The artist has skilfully cut the pale upper layer of the stone to suggest
the thin, transparent folds of the cloak held away from the body. This is well done
on another cameo in Naples attributed to Protarchos. Both our *nos 61* and *62* should
perhaps be associated with his œuvre. Hermaphrodite figures appear in Greek art
first in the Hellenistic period, which well exploited the sensual combination of the
slim adolescent male and female bodies. The motif on *no. 62*, where she uncovers
herself, is a rare one which is seen again on gems (all may not be ancient) and on
a painting in the Casa dei Vettii at Pompeii where a satyr leans over her shoulder
to admire her.

Erotes are not always about their mother's business, but they play a major part in the symbolism of early Roman art. Leaning weary or asleep on an upturned torch, they are common figures in Roman funerary art and on gems, as *no. 63*. Psyche, personification of the human soul, was represented as a young girl with butterfly wings, or could be replaced by a butterfly alone, a common soul-symbol. Where Eros hunts a butterfly, as on *no. 64*, the intention is obvious. These chubby putti are hardly mature enough to favour Psyche in the terms of the story, but this was no defect in symbolic scenes like this.

The Aphrodite wringing her hair dry on *no. 65* appears in the pose adopted from the famous kneeling Aphrodite by the third-century artist Doidalsas. This version is best known in the marble statue of the second or first century BC in Rhodes and was much copied in antiquity in various media.

From mortal subjects we have the possible Tiberius on *no. 66*, and the mother and child on *no. 67*. On *no. 68*, Story-Maskelyne took it that the woman was being led to a nocturnal sacrifice or festival but she seems less to be following than dispatching the girl who sets off with her torch and jug. Perhaps she is a young initiate going to participate in a ceremony by night. The scene is unique, the cutting extremely fine.

The satyr and maenad heads on *nos 69* and *70* bring us back to the Dionysiac motifs on the intaglios. There are mask cameos too, but *no.71* assembles an unusual composition of four masks, two satyric and two tragic, ranged on either side of the name of the great Athenian playwright Euripides, written in Greek letters. From the letter forms the earliest possible date for the cameo is the first century AD. The quality of the cutting of the masks suggests that it is no later. A Marlborough intaglio presents a similar composition of different masks, and the central name is Helena, in Latin, perhaps referring to Euripides' play. Dramatic masks, busts and whole figures of actors we have seen to be common devices on gemstones but this commemoration of a particular author or his work is rather unexpected.

Instead of the *grylloi* and animal heads of the engraved gems there are more individual animal studies on cameos, like the stork on *no.72*.

A few cameos of rather later date are cut somewhat more crudely. On *no.73* the deadly glance of Medusa is averted. The head is a late version of the Classical one, well copied very much later on *no. 98*. Leda reclines to receive the swan on *no.74*, the simple detail on both figures roughly cut. She stands to the swan in Classical art, but already in the fourth century on a gold ring is shown semi-recumbent, and this is the usual late pose, together with that copied on our *no. 84*. A thin translucent upper layer is exploited on *no.75* for the nymph's dress and hair-cloth.

42

She sits in a rustic sanctuary. The cutting is surer here but the body contorted to show the plump belly in a late manner, and the rocks cut so mechanically as to provide for her what seems a most insecure seat. The lyre-playing Eros of *no.76* is an awkward version of the plump putti we have seen on other cameos. As a lyre-player he is usually shown on Roman gems squatting with one leg tucked under him.

As well as the cameos which rely for their effect on the cutting of contrasting coloured strata in the stone, there are a number of gems cut in relief from monochrome or banded stones where the background is not differentiated by colour but by its more uniform translucency. Such is the comic mask on *no.77* where the high relief and polished bald head present the subject in a boldly decorative manner. This is clearly early Roman. Animal-head studies, such as the fine ram in agate, *no.78*, are more difficult to date. There are some roughly analogous ancient examples, like a lion-head relief in Vienna, and they do not seem to have found much favour with late copyists. The surface of our stone shows high polish and virtually no wear, but part of the edge had been broken away and it may have been repolished. The unpolished horn, hair and ear make an effective contrast with the bright surface of the flesh and background.

A hand tweaking an ear is a common gesture to request attention and recollection in Roman art and literature. A god pulls Virgil's ear to recall him to his duty of writing pastoral poetry rather than of kings and wars – *Cynthia aurem vellit [Eclogues* vi 3–4]. On *no.79* the gesture is accompanied by a lengthier inscription than most, 'Remember me, your dear sweetheart, and fare well Sophronios'. Gems like this might serve as pledges, given to dear ones going a journey, to a husband or lover away on military service. A very similar stone in London with the same representation asks, 'Remember me, your love, wherever you are', while on others without the hand and ear we read, 'They say what they like. Let them talk. I do not care. Kiss me; you'll like it!'. The lettering on these gems, cut in a very shallow relief, suggests a date no earlier than the fifth century AD. The other object shown on our gem may be a knotted diadem. Knots too have a magical significance, as well as being aids to remembrance, nowadays effected in handkerchiefs.

CHAPTER V

The Post-Antique

The later centuries of the Roman Empire saw a steady decline in interest in the miniaturist arts of the gem-engraver. Through the Middle Ages it was in France, it seems, that the techniques were remembered for gems with portraits or Christian devices, and it must not be forgotten that throughout this period ancient gems and cameos could be admired, set in jewellery or in various articles of furniture and religious ornaments. In the fourteenth century, Italian artists too take a hand in the production of engraved stones for personal signets or with Christian motifs, but the dominant style is still 'Gothic' and only after the later fifteenth century do classicizing subjects again appear. These follow closely the 'Classical' styles of the contemporary Renaissance arts, without especially copying ancient gems. The craft attracted the finest artists but there is no more danger of confusing their work with the ancient, than there is the sculpture of Michelangelo, however much the artists admired and copied ancient models. It is in the eighteenth century that ancient gems were themselves regularly copied, although they had already for long been assiduously collected. Publications of engravings made available a full range of subjects, and particular interest was shown in signed pieces, a demand the copyist was not slow to satisfy. Most were not, however, made to deceive although many were later passed by collectors and dealers as genuine. A considerable number bore the true names of their engravers, although often in Greek letters, and there were many strongly classicizing subjects which we should judge in the same terms as we judge the work of an artist like Canova. The gems were but another symptom of the age of neo-Classicism, of Wedgwood and Flaxman in England.

By 1800 there were flourishing studios working for royal or noble collectors in Italy, France, Germany and England. And for those who could not collect the gems themselves there were the cabinets of glass or coloured wax impressions made from the originals and published by the thousand. Raspe's catalogue (1791) of casts made by James Tassie numbers 15,800 pieces. The end of this prolific period of copying comes at about the time that the Elgin marbles reached London and the Aegina marbles Munich. Scholars and artists could see that there was more to ancient art than the Hellenistic and Roman styles which they and the Renaissance had known best. The engravers lost their patronage and perhaps their enthusiasm. Collecting continued, but more critically. The copyists' works were spurned, sometimes unjustly, and interest gradually turned to gems of the Archaic and true Classical periods, from Greece or Etruria. However, collectors still kept and acquired the more recent stones whether or not their real date was always recognized. A number of those in the Ionides Collection will be described in this chapter, and some of the criteria by which they may be discerned can be usefully first discussed.

The distinguishing features of the copyists' gems can be described in general terms but there are no universally sure criteria. It is still possible to make mistakes in dating: no doubt there are some in this book. The spirit of an age is reflected in its scholarship no less than in its dress or literature. Thirty or forty years ago only scepticism seemed proper to academic criticism, but nowadays scholars are more generous in their assessment of what is authentic, often assisted by science, but generally by a fuller understanding of ancient methods and fashions.

The late engraver is most easily recognized when he invents. The concocted iconography of the many gems in the notorious Poniatowsky Collection is an obvious example. Where he merely adapts it may be too easy for him to misunderstand the ancient conventions and introduce the wrong figure, the wrong dress or the wrong action. There is in particular a tendency to overload the scene with unnecessary properties or furniture, where the Classical artist would include only the essentials for the narrative or the composition. And he has often a sad inability to fill the available field, which was a notable skill of the ancient artist. When it comes to inscriptions the copyist likes his letters to be read, and does not appreciate the modest finesse of the tiny signatures of antiquity [contrast our *nos 18* and *80*]. Sometimes he simply mis-spells or invents impossible names. I am writing here of gems that were intended to deceive, either by the artist or the patron. Many, of course, by the best eighteenth-century engravers and in the purest classicizing styles were honestly and proudly signed.

Direct copies of ancient motifs from gems will carry no iconographic faults. Technically they may be detected by the near-mechanical, metallic cutting of details, betraying the harder tools and true lathes of a modern workshop. They look too good, too precise and they lack the spontaneous and confident appeal of an ancient work. But these are questions of taste, and judgement and opinions will differ. The surface of an ancient stone has generally been exposed to years of wear or handling and acquired a mass of tiny haphazard scratches over its polished surface which are readily detected under a glass. Attempts to simulate these signs of wear may be betrayed by the undue regularity of the marking on the stone. Some such attempts are blatant. Clearest, perhaps, are those where the surface has been roughened by the application of acid over part of the gem. The most ingenious method of introducing random markings was to make a turkey swallow the stone and let the gravel in its crop do the work. This effect was probably discovered through the examination of coloured stones which had been swallowed by poultry. Their appetite for bright stones is such that, according to S. H. Ball, the contents of the crops of chicken in the vicinity of a Colombian emerald mine are declared state property.

Eighteenth-century gems, whether or not they were intended to deceive, suffered little or no wear, and unless their surfaces were deliberately tampered with in one of the ways described, they will appear clear and brilliant under a glass. Even so, this cannot be a safe criterion. An ancient gem might reasonably have suffered little wear before interment, or it could have been re-polished in recent times, although if the re-polishing removed much of the surface this might be detected at the edges of the intaglio where the true original contour might be appreciably altered.

In matters of cutting techniques few clues are offered as they have changed so little since antiquity. On the harder stones, a drill and cutting wheel or point with a blunt or rounded end do most of the work of blocking out the figures. The cutting agent would be emery dust. In antiquity, the drill was probably a bow-operated hand drill working on the fixed stone, while the modern engraver works with a fixed lathe and moves the stone against the cutter. A clay lump in which he could take impressions would tell the artist how the modelling of the figure was developing. The final detail would be added by hand, but we see full and decorative use of the basic drilling techniques alone on Etruscan *a globolo* gems, as our *no. 8*. Finally comes the polishing which was never excessive on Greek stones (indeed it was unknown on the earlier Archaic gems), but a regular practice of the Italian studios, Etruscan and Roman, and of the modern. As magnifying aids rock-crystal lenses could have been used since the Bronze Age and clear glass lenses in the Roman period, but no certain examples have been found. The absence of specific reference to magnifying lenses in Pliny and other authors tells against any regular use of them by ancient artists. No doubt the magnifying effect of crystal or glass discs and inlays, or of clear glass bottles filled with water, was observed, and we know that their use as burning glasses was known, but without exact grinding or casting the images would have been too distorted to be of much use to the artist. The use of lenses by modern engravers seems not, however, to have introduced miniaturist work which surpasses the best of antiquity, at least on stones which might be taken for ancient. They are more likely to be detected through uneven detailing of a figure, lavishing their attention on features or hair while leaving limbs or drapery quite summary. This is a common fault of the latter-day forger. Ancient works, good and poor, observe what might be called a rule of uniformity in detail. The artist might be limited by his tools or his skill, and on occasion he chose to emphasize some features at the expense of others, but he did not display on one part of his work a degree of detail in tooling which was not to some extent exercised on the whole.

On the examples chosen for illustration with this chapter, the motifs are all classical and they will be discussed in terms of the ancient devices they were copying or adapting. Some are betrayed by their misunderstanding or abuse of ancient motifs [nos 82, 86, 94, 95]; some by their over-perfect [nos 80, 84, 85, 93, 94] or artificially damaged [nos 86, 91] surfaces; some by their inscriptions [nos 80, 81, 85]; some by more than one of these criteria, and all, in varying degrees, by their slick technique. Even so, it may prove that some should be promoted to earlier chapters or others relegated thence to this chapter. In no other major art of antiquity are true and false distinguished with such pain and uncertainty.

No. 80, in common with several late gems, bears the inscription SOTRATOU, 'by Sotratos': a mis-spelling of the name of the first-century BC artist Sostratos, which gives it an impossible form. The shallow hard cutting of the figure also suggests the stone's modernity but it is of high quality for its period and the pose is true to its models. The head recalls the portrait on early coins of Mark Antony, perhaps deliberately. If so, this would be an argument in favour of the antiquity of the gem, to which the inscription would have been later added. The stick with the snake which the youth holds is an abbreviated form of the staff usually carried by Asklepios and occasionally by other and minor healing heroes, who may be beardless. Or, perhaps the copyist has in mind Hermes, a suitable figure for this pose, and has unravelled the snakes of his caduceus.

The motif on *no. 81* has already been discussed *à propos* of its appearance on *no. 48*. This version closely copies the gem signed by Anteros, and the signature here – 'by Moschos' – is placed in the same position beneath the ground line. This is not a signature which seems otherwise recorded, and although Moschos is an ancient name it was probably chosen here for its meaning in Greek – a calf. The mottled stone of *no. 81* makes it impossible to view the device clearly in original, only in impression.

The hippocamp carrying the god on *no. 82* is of the same breed that serves to bear Nereids or even Eros, and a maenad on our *no. 28*. When similar elderly deities with a trident and on a sea-horse appear on Athenian vases of the sixth century BC, scholars prefer to name them Nereus. On coins of about 70 BC, Poseidon is carried on a chariot drawn by two of the creatures, but in Roman art he does not normally ride the beast: a fact unknown to the eighteenth-century engraver of our stone, which may have been made for Poniatowsky.

Several copies are known of the graceful study of a seated girl with a lyre, often identified as Sappho, *no. 83*. One is signed by Luigi Pichler, but it is not clear whether any ancient gem with this motif in this style had survived to be copied and it may rather have been inspired by Classical or classicizing reliefs.

To approach Leda (or Nemesis) in the guise of a swan, Zeus sent his eagle to seem to frighten the bird and win the girl's sympathy and protection. On *no. 84* the terrified bird runs to her embrace, while she holds her cloak protectively over them both. This copies a version seen on some ancient gems but it was by no means so popular as the act of love itself. The Hellenistic type of the crouching Aphrodite had been adapted for the figure of Leda.

Portraits are often copied or invented. *No. 85* shows a good head in the Roman manner, wrongly identified as Mark Antony by the inscription. The gem with the three heads, *no. 86*, presents more complex problems. It is not ancient, its surface has been artificially roughened, but it is an instructive example of the copyist's craft. A very similar stone was published by King in the last century in two poor and contradictory drawings, but there is an impression of it in Oxford. It was in the Muirhead collection, of sard, and King reports its provenience as Egypt in one place, India in another. The heads are clearly intended for portraits. King saw Ptolemy I, his wife Berenice and son Philadelpheus on the Muirhead stone, but the features do not closely match existing portraits. The way the hair of the farthest head is brushed back and caught in a fillet is only paralleled on portraits of the early Ptolemies, but never shown so ineptly. The second figure's hair style is a man's but, with a fillet, could be taken for a woman's. The near head wears a wreath like a

Roman emperor, such as was never worn on portraits of Ptolemies. Behind these stones there may well be a Ptolemaic family group, copied by an artist who failed to understand the hair styles and whose gratuitous addition of the wreath was a profound anachronism. The very idea of a three-head group is remarkable. Two heads shown in this manner were a Hellenistic type taken over by the Romans, and on coins of the Roman period we do see three heads in the scheme of our gem, for the Triumviri, Octavian, Antony and Lepidus, in 43 BC. The only evidence that the three-head group was also a Hellenistic device is seen in some clay impressions from seals found at Edfu in Egypt and dating to the Ptolemaic period. On one example three deities are shown, on the other, possibly, members of the royal family.

No. 87 offers a very popular motif on early Roman gems and with copyists. It is the bust from a herm, showing the square projections at the shoulders end on. The bearded head has butterfly wings sprouting behind the ears. He is often taken for Hypnos, the personification of Sleep, but Hypnos, although regularly shown with a winged head, is a youth. Furtwängler explained such heads as of Hermes in his role as god of sleep. Hermes it should certainly be, but rather as the guide of the souls of the dead, *psychopompos*. We see the soul-symbolism of butterflies or butterfly wings on other works, notably for the personification of the soul itself, Psyche. Recall the Eros with a butterfly on *no. 64*. The exchange of Hermes' usual feathered head-wings for butterfly wings is most readily thus explained. Winckelmann had thought to see Plato in these heads, the wings symbolizing his ideas about the immortality of the soul. The rather shallow, metallic cutting of the gem proclaims its late date.

The stone with the mask, *no. 88*, is described by Lippold as the work of Luigi Pichler, of the distinguished family of engravers. The rather trivial Graeco-Roman theme is treated with pretension. On *no. 89* the artist has rendered the long hair with brave abandon and may have intended an Alexander. *No. 90* is a far more mannered version of a youthful, almost Parisian, Dionysos with ivy crown. The more trivial Dionysiac themes and masks, *nos 91–3*, understandably retained their popularity. The young Dionysos on *no. 94* is a sleek and competent version of the common theme which we have already seen treated by Hyllos on *no. 31*. Another copy, of exactly this figure, is known, but it carries also an artist's signature, 'by Skymnos'. The name means 'whelp' in Greek and may have been adopted by an unknown late copyist in imitation of the artist Skylax, whose name has the same meaning. This modern Skymnos probably cut *no. 94* also.

Another popular Dionysiac motif on early Roman gems was the young satyr dancing, his head thrown back, holding thyrsos and animal skin, while an overturned wine bowl rolls on the ground at his feet. The figure alone is familiar on early Roman clay reliefs and relief vases, and there is a trivial version of the motif on a small ancient nicolo in the Ionides Collection [*no. 114*] not illustrated here. It is the same pose and attributes that we see for the figure of a dancing maenad on *no. 95*. She still carries a cup, however, her cymbals hang before her as from a tree, and a panther leaps by her side. The thyrsos is a wand or reed tipped by a bunch of ivy leaves which often resemble a pine cone. Maenads carry them by right, but so may satyrs or Dionysos. A two-ended thyrsos like the one our maenad carries is odd but to be seen on Campana reliefs where it is carried by a satyr or Dionysos. Our artist has added this oddity to a superfluity of other Dionysiac equipment, setting the figure loosely in the field.

A sophisticated and sympathetic eighteenth-century rendering of a more sober motif on late Hellenistic and early Roman gems is the elderly Dionysos with thyrsos and mug on *no. 96*.

A common variant of the animal-head combinations seen on *nos 50, 51* was the conjunction of a human and a boar's head, such as is copied on *no. 97*. The human head is, however, generally bearded on the ancient gems and to be identified as a satyr.

Cameos have enjoyed more persistent popularity than intaglio gems. Two good late examples are shown here. The large Medusa of *no. 98* is a fine rendering of the Classical type of the Medusa Rondanini [see *p. 31*]. The smaller round cameo with Eros and a cock, *no. 99*, is still in its seventeenth- or eighteenth-century setting. The cock is a love-gift but also a fighting bird, so Eros may be shown in a friendly match with one.

CHAPTER VI

The Ionides Collection

The collection used to illustrate this account of engraved gems was made by Constantine Alexander Ionides (1833–1900) and his son, Alexander Constantine (1862–1931). The father was a connoisseur of wide interests and expertise, as can be judged from the quality of his bequest to the Victoria and Albert Museum, where a gallery bears his name. His son writes (in *Ion: A Grandfather's Tale*, privately published in Dublin, 1927) that his father began collecting 'originally, I believe, under the spell of his great-grandfather's will'. This had enjoined on his son that one-third of his fortune should be spent, one-third given to charity, and one-third set aside. It was in fact all sequestered by the Turks, and the family's fortunes were rebuilt in Britain, where the Ionides were senior members of the distinguished Greek community in London. Their interest in the arts, successfully combined with business acumen, was remarked by the rest of the community, which was dominantly Chiot, and the adverb *ionidika* was coined as a kindly description for any scheme which seemed unprecedented or unconventional. It was a usage of which the family could feel proud.

This was a period (only recently passed) in which the major collectors were also dealers, and objects passed from hand to hand within a comparatively limited circle, with profit or loss observed at each exchange. Count Tysckiewicz's memoirs describe the process vividly. Constantine kept himself apart from this dealing and preferred the company of artists and scholars. He was something of an autocrat: 'Zeus' to his family and friends. The family motto had been carried with them to

England – αἰὲν ἀριστεύειν – 'always to be the best'. In Homer, this command had been given Glaukos by his father, and it is recalled just before he is tricked by Zeus into exchanging his golden armour for Diomedes' bronze. Constantine Ionides was no Glaukos in his collecting as the extremely high quality of his cabinet of gems attests. His son improved the collection with further purchases and it is now owned by his great-grand-daughter.

Most of the gems were acquired in the nineteenth century, and the history of their former homes is in itself a history of gem-collecting, especially in England. In the early seventeenth century the Duke of Arundel was one of the first English-men to travel and collect antiquities not only in Italy but also in the Aegean world. His sculptures, after many vicissitudes and much reduction in number, are in Ox-ford. His collection of gems also passed through several hands, but was still intact when it was acquired by the Third Duke of Marlborough who, in the later eigh-teenth century, built up a notable collection of both ancient and Renaissance stones. This was sold, first in 1875, to David Bromilow, then in 1899, when the collection was dispersed. Ionides bought a dozen pieces, three of them Arundel's [*nos 60, 62, 68*]. The great portrait of Augustus [*no. 19*] had been bought by Marlborough for 23 guineas through Nathaniel Marchant, himself a distinguished gem-engraver. It is said once to have belonged to Winckelmann.

Many of the other gems are from a collection about whose ancestry little is known. It was made by a Mexican connoisseur called Rosarena (variously spelled Arosarena, Rosana, even Arizona!), and was dispersed after the middle of the nine-teenth century. Some of his gems were from the collections of Dr Nott and B. Hertz, well-known cabinets from which Ionides also acquired some pieces. Others were from the notorious Poniatowsky collection, the nucleus of which had been formed by the last King of Poland, Stanislaus, then added to by his nephew Prince Poniatowsky who acquired some 3,000 newly made gems by contemporary en-gravers. These were lavish with mythological scenes and inscriptions, and both Poniatowsky and the Englishman who bought much of the collection in the mid-nineteenth century insisted on their authenticity. Remnants of the collection were being sold for charity through Tiffanys early in this century. Where the works of these copyist engravers of the eighteenth and early nineteenth centuries were passed as originals they may legitimately be dubbed forgeries, but many are still consum-mate examples of the engraver's art, and no less those acquired by Poniatowsky. Our *no. 82* may have been in his collection, while *nos 83* and *88* may be the work of Luigi Pichler (1773–1854) of a distinguished family of master-engravers. Of these, *no. 83* was obtained by Ionides from the Rosarena collection, it seems, and he ac-

54

quired over thirty of the Mexican's gems, including some of the most important in his collection.

Of other sources the most notable was the Beugnot Collection, first sold in 1840, which yielded our *nos 1* and *2* after passing through other hands. It was only in the years before his death in 1900 that Ionides' gems became at all well known, and the collection, then in Brighton, was visited by scholars. Furtwängler had seen impressions of some pieces which he mentions in his great survey of ancient gems, and Arthur Evans had wax impressions of many of them. After Constantine's death a number were displayed in the Exhibition of Greek Art assembled by the Burlington Fine Art Club in 1903.

Alexander Ionides' purchases were fewer but no less distinguished than his father's. The story of his loss in a Swiss cesspool of a gold ring given him by his mother and subsequent recovery of it twenty years later in a field, is in a true heroic tradition. He acquired several gems from the collection of Charles Newton-Robinson, sold in 1909, and some from the sale in 1905 of part of the collection of the indefatigable Arthur Evans whose attentions were then engaged by his work in Crete, to which his own interest in engraved gems had first led him. One of the Ionides gems, not in the collection today, belonged formerly to Fenerli, physician to the Sultan in Istanbul. It had presumably been given to the younger Ionides, whose mother was a Fenerli, and whose maternal uncle was the selfsame physician to Abdul Hamid. He had visited him in Istanbul and commented on his 'safe deposit' of antiquities, including a 'head of Demeter', later sold to Castellani for £400, and eventually bought by the British Museum [Smith, *no. 1829*] for £10,000. The visit was an occasion for possible adventure too. The doctor said 'if I would like to impersonate a medical student, I could accompany him on his rounds through the Sultan's, and other, harems. – I asked him what risks were incurred. He told me. I wasn't taking any.'

The Plates

The stones and impressions are shown here at approximately four times life size, with the exception of the views of scarabs and the impression of No. 19. The last page of the plates shows a selection of the stones at life size.

The scale of the colour plates is not uniform. Exact measurements are given in the catalogue following the plates.

Nos. 4, 11, 32, 33, 48, 55 and 81 are shown in impression only.

1   1

2   2

3   3

4   5

6

7

1   2

6   7

9

8

10

13

13

11

12

15

14   16

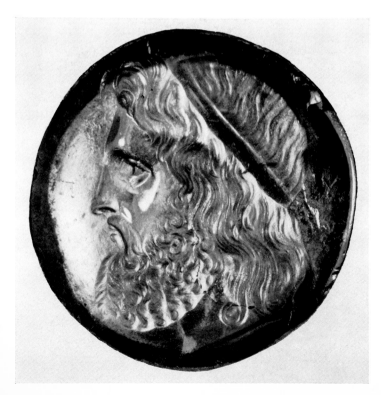

15

17   17

18   18

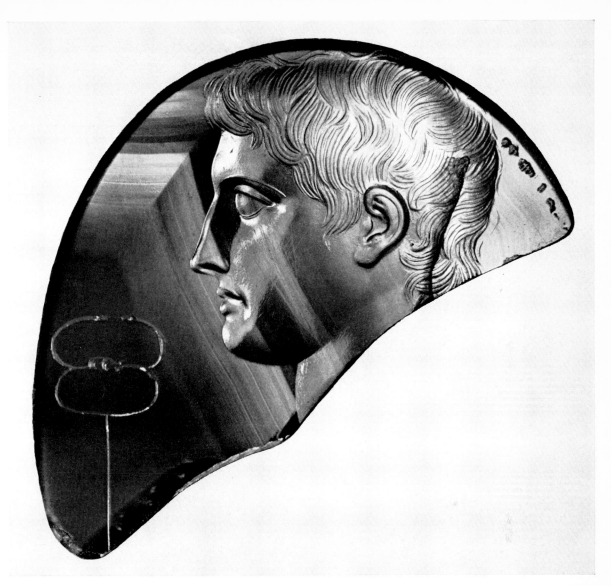

19

19

20

21

23

22

24

25

26

27 a

27 b

28

29   30

32

31

33

34

37

35

36   38

39 40

41

42

43

44

45

46

47   48   49

50   51

52

53   54

55

56

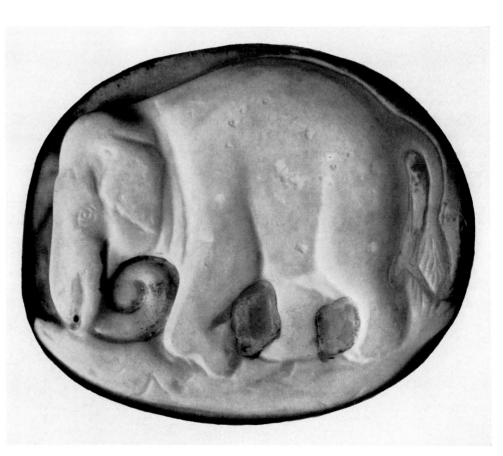

57

58

59

60

62

61

63

64

66

65

67

68

69

70

71

72

73

74

75

77

76

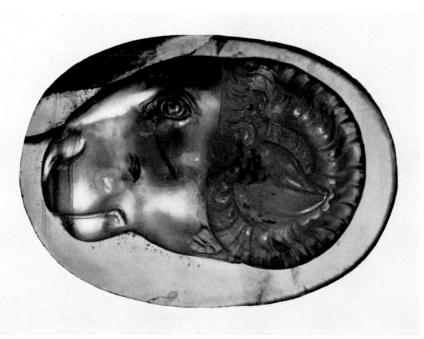

78

79

80   81

82

83

84   85

86   87

88

89

94 96

97

95

98

99

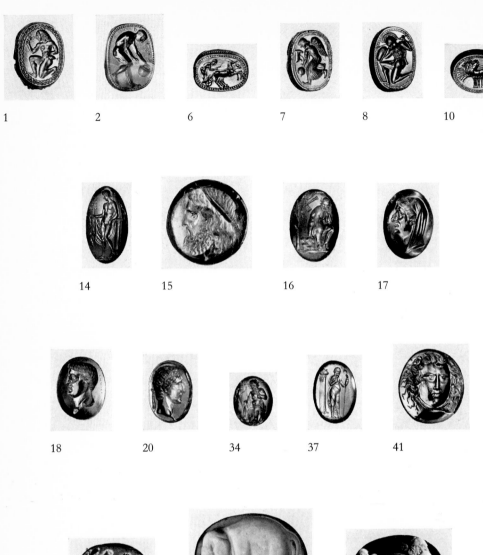

1   2   6   7   8   10

14   15   16   17

18   20   34   37   41

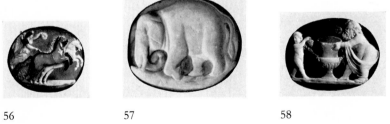

56   57   58

A SELECTION AT LIFE SIZE

THE IONIDES COLLECTION

Catalogue and Notes

CATALOGUE AND NOTES

The bracketed numbers refer to the Ionides Collection handlist. The major measurement of the face of each stone is given in millimetres.

1 (1) Cornelian scarab. 16.5 mm. The beetle has a stippled head, hatched border to the thorax, double-v winglets and a spine.
A running youth with cup and jug, in a cable border.
Formerly in the Beugnot Collection. *AG* pl. 8.19; Lippold, pl. 59.1; Beazley and Ashmole, *Greek Sculpture and Painting* fig. 216.
For this hair style: Eckstein in *Antike Plastik* i 47 ff.

2 (2) Onyx scarab. 18 mm. The beetle has a stippled head, hatched border to the thorax and tongue pattern on the vertical border.
A youth stoops to pick up a round-bottomed urn, in a hatched border. Inscription – ΚΑΣΤVΡ. The 'K' lacks an upright, like a *gamma*.
Formerly in the Beugnot Collection. *AG* pl. 17.44; Lippold, pl. 40.3.
For another example of this motif, Micali, *Storia* pl. 116.21 [Cades, Centuria i 46, Demidoff Collection]. On the scene, *AG* ii 84.

3 (114) Onyx scaraboid, with a hatched border on the back. 7 mm.
A girl-cock, in a pellet border.
AG pl. 6.68.
Archaic girl-cocks on Attic Tyrrhenian vases, *AJA* xlviii (1944) 164; on a Greek electrum coin in Oxford; on the fourth-century Metrodoros stele from Chios, Kekulé, *Beschreibung der antiken Skulpturen* (Berlin) no.766 A, figs on pp. 289–91.

4 (79) Cornelian ringstone. 17 mm. Convex face, flat back.
Eros flying with lyre and wreath, in a hatched border.
Formerly in the Robinson Collection [no. 20. pl.].
On similar motifs of this date, Beazley, *LHG* 28.

5 (3) Cornelian scarab. 13 mm. The beetle has a hatched border to the thorax, v-wing-lets and hatching on the vertical border.
A squatting negro boy, with oil bottle and strigil, on a ground line and in a hatched border.
Formerly in the Morrison [no. 41] and Robinson [no. 8] Collections. *AG* pl. 63.2; *BFAC* pl. 10.M 131; Lippold, pl. 66.8.
For the subject on gems, *AG* pl. 10.26, 28.

6 (5) Cornelian scarab. 14.5 mm. The beetle has a hatched border to the thorax, scrolls on the elytra (wing-cases) and hatching on the vertical border.
Two-horse chariot driven by a naked man holding a branch, in a hatched border.
Formerly in the Morrison and Robinson [no. 11, pl.] Collections. *BFAC* pl. 110.O 88.

7 (9) Cornelian scarab from Tarquinia. 15.5 mm. The beetle has a hatched border to the thorax, fine winglets and upright tongues on the vertical border.
A winged goddess wearing a chiton fills a water jug at the lion-head spout of a fountain. The border is hatched.
Formerly in the Evans Collection [no. 36, pl. 3].
For the same subject, *AG* pl. 20.11 [cornelian scarab, Southesk Collection].

8 (119) Cornelian scarab. 17 mm. The beetle has a hatched border to the thorax, v-wing-lets and hatching on the vertical border.
A kneeling, striking warrior, with helmet, cuirass, shield and spear, in a hatched border.
Formerly in the Morrison [no. 58] and Robinson [no. 11, pl. 17] Collections. *AG* pl. 63.26; *BFAC* pl. 110.M 143.

9 (8) Cornelian scarab. 11 mm. The beetle has a straight, hatched border to the thorax, triple oblique lines for winglets and narrow hatching on the vertical border.
A kneeling warrior with helmet, shield and spear, in a hatched border.
By the same hand, the scarab, *AG* pl. 20.57, following work like *AG* pl. 18.63–5.

10 (4) Cornelian scarab. 13.5 mm. The beetle is summary; it has a hatched border to the thorax, oblique double lines for the winglets and a hatched vertical border.
Victory driving her four-horse chariot, holding a whip. A ground line and hatched border.
For the motif on coins, e.g., *BMC Coins of the Roman Republic* pl. 83.12.

11 (15) Cornelian ringstone. 10.5 mm. Lightly convex face, flat polished back. A stag, raising a rear leg to scratch its belly, in a hatched border.
BFAC pl. 112.O 56. The same motif on ringstones in Baltimore [*Archaeology* 1962, 123, fig. 5; *BFAC* pl. 90.M 150; once Robinson, no. 30, pl.]; and *Berlin* 339, pl. 7. Also the cameo, below, *no. 118*. Cf. *New York* on 107.

12 (63) Garnet ringstone. 11 mm. Flat face, convex back.
Elderly man squatting, wearing a fillet and loin cloth, and holding the ritual *lituus*. In a hatched border.
Formerly in the Story-Maskelyne Collection [Sotheby, 4/5. vii. 1921, pl. 2.69]; King, *Ancient Gems and Rings* pl. 37.11; *BFAC* pl. 108.M 8.

13 (12) Glass gem, banded black and white, in its original gold ring. 11 mm.
Warrior with helmet, shield and spear, and short cloak, in a pellet border.
Impronti dell'Istituto M.10.
For just this style see *London* 1056, pl. 16.

14 (70) Cornelian ringstone. 20 mm. Convex face, flat back.
Apollo, with a cloak and holding a laurel branch, rests his elbow on a column which supports a tripod with a fillet tied to one of its legs. Ground line.

15 (103) Amethyst ringstone. 22.5 mm. Flat face, convex back.
Head of a bearded god, probably Poseidon, wearing a fillet. At either side the letters ΥΠ.
Formerly in the Rosarena Collection. King, *Handbook* 279, n. ('brought from India'); *BFAC* pl. 112.O 55 ('from India').
Head of Poseidon on coins of Antigonos Doson (229–20 BC), *BM Guide to the Principal Coins of the Greeks* pl. 35.4.

16 (71) Jacinth ringstone. 19 mm. Convex face, flat back.
A bald satyr seated in a pensive pose beside a tree on which hang his bagpipes and syrinx. Ground line.
For Marsyas groups see *AG* pl. 42.56, 28 [Lippold, pl. 9.5, 8]; eighteenth-century versions are *London* (Dalton) 706, pl. 25; Lippold, pl. 108.4.

17 (51) Amethyst ringstone. 17 mm. Convex face with a high-domed back.
Veiled head of an elderly woman.
Formerly in the Rosarena Collection. *AG* pl. 31.22; Lippold, pl. 69.6.
Furtwängler, in *AG* ii 154, suggests this is the portrait of the elderly Arsinoe II. For her portraits see Thompson in *American Journal of Archaeology* lix (1955) 199 ff.; Vollenweider, 14–16. The type, with veil, was adopted by the Romans for their goddess Vesta.

18 (36) Amethyst ringstone. 16.5 mm. Convex face, formerly with a domed back, partly now cut flat.
Head of Mark Antony. Inscribed ΓΝΑΙΟC.
Formerly in the Rosarena Collection.
On Gnaios, Vollenweider, 45–6, pls 41–3. Portraits of Antony in this style: Vessberg, *Studien* 156 ff., Type III, pl. 10.6–8. Good example on a coin, Cappelli, *Profili*

imperiali romani fig. 6. On gems, perhaps copies of ours, King, *Handbook* pl. 74.5 [sard, Marlborough Collection, Story-Maskelyne no. 378]; King, *Ancient Gems and Rings* pl. 48.11 (the illustration as the last, but as of the Capranesi Collection); *Archaeology* 1955, 257, fig. 7; Evans, *Selection of Greek Gems* pl. 7.151; and cf. *London* 1966, pl. 25 [*AG* pl. 47.31]. In Egypt, *American Journal of Archaeology* lx (1956) 330f. Portrait of a queen by Gnaios: Vollenweider, pl. 43.1–3. On 'Gaios' names see Fraser in *Berytus* xiii (1960) 146.

19 (113) Agate intaglio. 45 mm. Flat face and back.
Head of Augustus, with a caduceus.
Formerly in the Marlborough [ii pl. 16; Story-Maskelyne no. 387] and Robinson [no. 64, pl.] Collections. *AG* pl. 38.30, 40.32; *BFAC* pl. 110.O 86; *Römische Mitteilungen* xlii (1927) 174, fig. 3; Vollenweider, 53 f., pl. 53.1 [the companion piece, pl. 52.1].
Horace, *Carmina* i.2 25–6, 41–4. On Augustus as Mercury, Scott in *Hermes* lxiii (1928) 15 ff.; Brendel in *Römische Mitteilungen* l (1935) 231 ff. On Hermes and Emperors, Chittenden in *Numismatic Chronicle* 1945 41 ff.

20 (32) Sapphire ringstone. 16.5 mm. Convex face. Set in a fine sixteenth-century Italian gold ring with niello inlay.
Head of Augustus, with radiate crown.
Formerly in the Rosarena Collection.
For such heads see *AG* iii 317.

21 (69) Cornelian ringstone. 14 mm. Convex face, flat back.
Frontal view of a seated Zeus, holding sceptre and patera (?). On the throne back a small winged figure. On the left of the throne an eagle.
Formerly in the Nott and Rosarena Collections.
On Jupiter Capitolinus see *Journal of Roman Studies* xxviii (1938) 50ff. Winged figures on throne backs: Richter, *Ancient Furniture* figs 50, 51, 54, 67.

22 (38) Emerald ringstone. 11.5 mm. Convex face, flat back with bevelled edges.
Three-quarter facing head of Zeus Ammon.
Some examples of this common type: *London* 1278, pl. 18; *Berlin* 4838, pl. 35 and 6925, pl. 51 [*AG* pl. 41.3]; *New York* 260–1, pl. 38; Fossing, *Antique Engraved Gems: Thorwaldsen Museum* 1033, pl. 13; Lippold, pl. 2.3.

23 (65) Cornelian ringstone. 13.5 mm. Flat face and back with bevelled edges.
Profile bust of Sarapis.

24 (66) Garnet ringstone. 9.5 mm. High convex face and deep concave back; a carbuncle.
Facing head of Sarapis.
For this type in sculpture see Adriani, *Repertorio* A. ii 41 ff.

25 (83) Cornelian ringstone. 12 mm. Convex face, flat back with bevelled edges.
Bust from a herm. A bearded head wearing a fillet.
Busts of Jupiter Terminalis on coins: Sydenham, pl. 27.1034.

26 (89) Cornelian ringstone. 15 mm. Convex face and back.
Fortuna with cornucopia, branches and steering oar, dressed in chiton and himation.
Ground line.

27 (120) Sardonyx intaglio and cameo. 12 mm. A. convex face. B. white on brown.
A. Young male deity with sceptre, holding a fruit (?) and wearing a *hmhm* crown.
B. Pantheos – child with radiate head, disc-and-horn crown and winged heels,
holding a thunderbolt and cornucopia.
Formerly in the Rosarena Collection.
For the figure on B see *AG* pl. 43.56. Daremberg-Saglio, *Dictionnaire* s.v. 'Panthea
signa'; Paulys *Realencyclopädie* s.v. 'Pantheion' viii.

28 (68) Cornelian ringstone. 17 mm. Flat face with shallow convex back.
A maenad holding a thyrsos riding over the sea supported by a hippocamp and a dolphin.
Formerly in the Morrison [no. 75] and Evans [no. 64, pl. 5] Collections.
Some Nereids on hippocamps: London 1299, pl. 18; 3725, pl. 33; *AG* pl. 41.39;
Berlin 3645–7, pl. 29.

29 (109) Gold ring with engraved bezel. 12 mm. The simple broad hoop is flat on the
inside, curved outside.
Eros holding a trident rides a dolphin. Two fish below.
Eros on a dolphin on coins of *c.* 74 BC: Sydenham, pl. 22.784. With trident on a
Campana relief, Rohden-Winnefeld, 25, fig. 42; a mosaic, Reinach, *Répertoire de
Peintures* 36.3; a gem, once Evans, no. 65, pl. 5.

30 (34) Topaz ringstone. 11 mm. Convex face, bevelled domed back.
Three-quarter facing head of Heracles, with short hair, bushy beard.
Formerly in the Rosarena Collection.

31 (81) Cornelian ringstone. 19.5 mm. Shallow convex face, flat back.
The drunken Dionysos, with cloak and animal skin, holding thyrsos and jug. Inscribed VΛΛ. Ground line.
For the pose compare *AG* pl. 36.34 [Lippold, pl. 11.6]; *Berlin* 6238, pl. 42; and
many late copies as our *no. 94*; *London* (Dalton) 692–3, pl. 25. On Hyllos see Vollenweider, 69 ff.

32 (43) Emerald ringstone. 10.5 mm. Diamond-shaped with low pyramidal back.
Three-quarter facing bust of a youthful Dionysos, wreathed with ivy and bunches
of grapes.

Formerly in the Rosarena and Hertz Collections. *BFAC* pl. 112.O 54.

Compare a gem once in the Robinson Collection [no. 63, pl.; Marlborough no. 212; *BFAC* pl. 90.M 182]; and heads on Campana reliefs, Rohden-Winnefeld, 31 and pl. 31.1.

33 (35) Garnet ringstone. 13 mm. High convex face, flat back.
Facing head of a youthful Dionysos with vine wreath.

34 (76) Cornelian ringstone. 13 mm. Convex face, the back rough and cut flat.
A wreathed satyr with a thyrsos, seated and holding a cup to his lips.
Formerly in the Nott and Rosarena Collections. King, *Ancient Gems and Rings* pl. 30.1; Lippold, pl. 14.4.
Compare Fossing, *Antique Engraved Gems: Thorwaldsen Museum* 795, pl. 10.

35 (42) Cornelian ringstone. 11 mm. Low convex face, domed back.
Facing bust of a bald wreathed satyr.
For rather similar types see *Berlin* 1108, pl. 14; *London* 1569, pl. 21; Lippold, pl. 111.5 (as modern).

36 (62) Cornelian ringstone. 11 mm. Flat face, convex back.
Pan, with goat's legs and tail, seated shouldering a thyrsos and contemplating a mask.
Formerly in the Marlborough Collection [Story-Maskelyne no. 239].
For the motif compare *Impronti dell'Istituto* II.A 385; Collection Duval, *Arethusa* ii (1925) pl. 5.30. On Pan, Dionysos and the theatre, Herbig, *Pan* 30f.

37 (90) Cornelian ringstone. 16.5 mm. Convex face, flat back.
Masked comic actor wearing a himation and holding a crooked stick beside a pillar on which there is a tragic mask. He tugs at his beard.
Formerly in the Nott and Rosarena Collections. *AG* pl. 41.50; Lippold, pl. 60.3. This whole group on the Vienna cameo, Kris-Eichler, *Kameen* pl. 12.63. For the figure without the column compare *London* 3630, pl. 42; *AG* pl. 41.48 [Lippold, pl. 60.1], 49; *LHG* pl. 7.108.

38 (125) Onyx ringstone. 24 mm. Flat face with bevelled sides, flat back.
An actor wearing a mask, dressed in a long-sleeved tunic and cloak, seated on an altar.

39 (25) Nicolo ringstone. 10.5 mm. Bevelled front and back.
Comic mask of a woman.
Formerly in the Rosarena Collection.

40 (75) Topaz ringstone. 9.5 mm. Convex face and domed back.
Facing mask of a grotesque bald bearded man.

For this type compare *Berlin* 7026, pl. 52; Marlborough ii additional pl.; *London* 1580, pl. 21 [Lippold, pl. 153.11, as modern].

41 (40) Garnet ringstone. 18.5 mm. High convex face with a deep concave back; a carbuncle. The lower edge broken away.
Facing head of Medusa, snakes knotted beneath the chin.
Formerly in the Rosarena Collection.
For this general type compare *London* 1831, 1833, pl. 23. On the Hellenistic type, Buschor, *Medusa Rondanini* 17 ff.

42 (67) Pale cornelian ringstone. 12.5 mm. Flat face and back.
Facing head of Medusa, with wings in her hair, as centrepiece to a triskeles with one leg in retreat, and three ears of corn.
Formerly in the Rosarena Collection.
Other examples of the motif on gems: Evans Collection, no. 127, pl. 9; *Berlin* 6616, pl. 47 [*AG* pl. 26.74; Lippold, pl. 98.17]; *New York* 557, pl. 63. On coins of *c.* 49 BC: Sydenham, 171, pl. 27.1029. The reversed leg on a shield device on an Etruscan black figure vase, Langlotz, *Griechische Vasen in Würzburg* pl. 232. An early gorgoneion with triskeles, perhaps, Gerhard, *Auserlesene Vasenbilder* pl. 141.3.

43 (52) Cornelian ringstone. 14 mm. Convex face.
Profile head and three-quarter back view of the shoulders of a woman with long loose hair. Behind her head the crescent moon.
Formerly in the Bessborough and Marlborough [Story-Maskelyne no.320] Collections. For the motif on gems, Vollenweider, 26, n. 7; on coins, Sydenham, pl. 23. 796 A [*c.* 70 BC]. For the Selene phalera, Vollenweider, 25 and pl. 14.2, remarking that she was Sulla's goddess. On the three-quarter back motif: Möbius, *Alexandria und Rom* 19–23.

44 (74) Cornelian ringstone. 14 mm. Flat face and back.
Aeneas shoulders his father Anchises and leads his son (Ascanius or Julus) from Troy. Beneath him a cicada (?). Ground line.
Formerly in the Rosarena Collection. *Impronti dell'Istituto* C 3.
The group on mid-first-century BC coins without the child: Sydenham, pl. 27.1013, and *Archaeology* 1949, 35. On gems, Vollenweider, 17 f., n. 6. Closest to ours is Evans, no. 92, pl. 6.

45 (45) Garnet ringstone. 19 mm. High convex face, deep concave back; a carbuncle.
Ganymede, seated on a rock, offers a cup to the eagle. He wears a skin cap and chlamys. Behind him a tree arching over the group. Ground line.
The group without the tree on the cameo, *London* 3423, pl. 33. On Ganymede feeding the eagle see Sichtermann, *Ganymed* 69 f., 93–5; for this pose, *ibid.*, pl. 15.2. With Eros: Hackin, *Begram, Nouvelles Recherches* 123–6. Another example, Burton Y. Berry

97

Collection 76 (Indiana University Publications 5). For Venus and the eagle in this scheme, Vollenweider, pl. 96.7–10. On a coin of Troy: *BMC Coins, Troas, etc.* pl. 12.8; on a sarcophagus, *Die antiken Sarkophagreliefs* ii pl. 2.3, 4; at Pompeii, Helbig, *Wandgemälde* no. 154, cf. 158 [Reinach, *Répertoire de Peintures* 14.8, 9].

46 (24) Nicolo ringstone. 12 mm. Bevelled face with flat back.
Diomedes with drawn sword is climbing across the altar, lifting the Palladion from its pillar. A ship's prow (?) beyond the altar.
For this scheme of the popular motif see Vollenweider, 51, n. 24 and pl. 47.5, 6, 8; Hackin, op. cit., 130–3; on a sarcophagus, *Die antiken Sarkophagreliefs* ii pl. 51.139a. Signed examples of the other versions, Vollenweider, pls 39.1–2, 41, 49.1, 62.

47 (27) Nicolo ringstone. 10 mm. Bevelled face, flat back.
A bearded man (Odysseus) in a pensive posture, resting on a staff and seated on a roller. Lightly incised inscription ΔΙΟΓΗΝΕΣ, modern.
Formerly in the Marlborough Collection, Story-Maskelyne no. 343.
For this scene see *AG* ii 127; with Penelope, pl. 25.36 [Lippold, pl. 44.3], and Vollenweider, pl. 66.6. At Pompeii: Herrmann, *Denkmäler der Malerei des Altertums* 69–71, pls 54–5. Helbig, *Wandgemälde* no. 201 [Reinach, *Répertoire de Peintures* 28.5] for Hermes seated on a roller.

48 (39) Topaz ringstone. 10.5 mm. Convex face, domed back.
A wreathed youth carries a calf on his shoulder.
For the version by Anteros see Vollenweider, pls 38.1, 40.1; on pastes, *Berlin* 4189–92, pl. 31; on a Boston gem, *AG* pl. 50.22; on a glass vase, *Rev. Arch.* 1879.i pl. 7; on a cameo, *The Beverley Gems* no. 32; on a Campana relief, Rohden-Winnefeld, pl. 47. Cf. *AG* ii 236.

49 (131) Pale cornelian ringstone. 8 mm. Flat back.
A boy holding a branch plays or fights with two cocks.
The group with an Eros: *London* 1506, pl. 20; *AG* pl. 42.41, 47 [*Berlin* 6789, pl. 49].

50 (82) Cornelian ringstone. 13 mm. Convex face, flat back.
Grotesque composed of a peacock, bearded head and elephant's head. Ground line. Inscribed NICE T.P.S.A.
Formerly in the Marlborough Collection, Story-Maskelyne no. 686. *AG* pl. 65.20. Very similar are Evans, no. 96, pl. 6; *AG* pls 29.59, 46.37 [Lippold, pl. 83.14, 12]. The motto latinizes Greek *nike*.

51 (77) Cornelian ringstone. 10 mm. Shallow convex face and back.
Grotesque composed of a cock, a bearded head, a flower and a ram's head with an ear of corn (?) in its mouth. Ground line.

Impronti dell' Istituto 31.

Very similar are *Berlin* 7821, pl. 57; *London* 2576, pl. 29. The Stratos mould: *Bulletin de Correspondance Hellénique* lxxxix (1965) 760, fig. 1. On grotesques of this type, Roes in *Journal of Hellenic Studies* lv (1935) 232–5.

52 (87) Cornelian ringstone. 11 mm. Flat face and back.
Grouped heads of a bull, goat, boar and ram, with an ear of corn (?).
Most similar are *AG* pl. 46.27 [Lippold, pl. 83.10]; *The Beverley Gems* no. 92.

53 (31) Amethyst ringstone. 13.5 mm. Convex face and domed back.
Laureate head of an emperor. Inscribed ΦΩΤΙΟΥ ΑΘΗ.
Impronti dell' Istituto C 445.

54 (86) Cornelian ringstone. 12 mm. Flat face and back.
Bearded laureate head of Pescennius Niger.
Impronti dell' Istituto C 550.
Compare coins of Niger, AD 193–4: *BMC Coins of the Roman Empire* iv pls 13–14.7; Cappelli, *Profili imperiali romani* fig. 60.

55 (33) Emerald ringstone. 14.5 mm. Convex face, domed back. Badly damaged surface.
Heads of a man and a woman.
Formerly in the Rosarena Collection.
A similar couple of this period: Gori i 14.10 [Reinach, pl. 9]. A little later is *London* 2023, pl. 25.

56 (95) Sardonyx cameo, white on brown. 21 mm. Flat back.
Victory holding a wreath drives a two-horse chariot. Ground line.
On the type, Vollenweider, 34, n. 48.

57 (100) Sardonyx cameo, ivory on yellowish-brown ground. 30.5 mm. Flat back. An elephant tramples and gores a fish.
Formerly in the Marlborough Collection, Story-Maskelyne no. 705. *BFAC* pl. 112.O 61.
On Caesar and elephant coins: Sydenham, 167, pl. 27.1006; Swindler, *American Journal of Archaeology* xxvii (1923) 308 f.; Aurigemma, *Africa Italiana* vii (1940) 70–2. For bull and wolf coins of the Social War: Sydenham, pl. 19.628, 641. Crocodile versus hippo, on the base of the Vatican Nile, Adriani, *Repertorio* A. ii pl. 90 (pulling its snout); on the gem, Smith and Hutton, *Catalogue of the Wyndham Francis Cook Collection* ii pl. 8.352 (trampling); attacking a cow whose master is pulling her back by her tail, in mosaic in the 'Cathedral' at Cyrene, and a donkey, similarly aided, in mosaic at El Alia, *Inventaire des Mosaiques* ii (Tunisie) no. 93. On elephants and serpents, Hecksher in *Art Bulletin* xxix (1947) 160.

58 (96) Sardonyx cameo, white on red-brown. 25 mm. Flat back.
Plump wreathed Silenus at a crater, with a child bearing grapes. Ground line.
BFAC pl. 112.O 58.
For Sostratos see Vollenweider, 32 ff., pls 23–7.

59 (14) Sardonyx cameo, white on brown. 10 mm. Flat back.
Sacrifice scene. At the left an old satyr blows his pipes; at the centre a woman holding a tray stoops over an altar to which, from the right, a man leads a ram for sacrifice. Behind the woman is a pillar supporting an image of Priapus.
Formerly in the Rosarena Collection. *BFAC* pl. 112.O 60.
For this motif see *AG* pls 46.13, 64.23 (gem and cameo in Vienna).

60 (21) Onyx cameo, white on dark grey. 12 mm.
Two Erotes erect a trophy, already dressed in helmet and cuirass, the shield waiting on the ground.
Formerly in the Marlborough Collection, ii pl. 41, Story-Maskelyne no. 157.
For the motif see *New York* 306, pl. 42; Gori i pl. 74.9 [Reinach, pl. 36]; Fossing, *Thorwaldsen Museum* 778, pl. 10; Kassel, *Arch. Anzeiger* 1965, 65, no. 34; on the frieze of the Temple of Venus Genetrix, *Memoirs of the American Academy in Rome*, xiii pl. 51.1 and *Enciclopedia dell' Arte antica* iii 433, fig. 527. Eros bound to the trophy, Vollenweider, pl. 33.1–2. Compare the work of Tryphon, *ibid.*, pl. 28.1–2.

61 (30) Nicolo cameo, pale blue on deep blue-grey. 19.5 mm. Highly polished.
Eros rides a horse. Ground line.
Formerly in the Morrison Collection [no. 4].
For Eros on a horse in this pose: *AG* pl. 35.28 [Lippold, pl. 26.5]; Smith and Hutton, *Catalogue of the Wyndham Francis Cook Collection* ii pl. 7.145; Toronto, *Lock Collection* 56 no. 186. On early representations of the subject, Beazley in *Boston Vases* iii 89. Naked winged figures on horses on Clazomenian sarcophagi [*Antike Denkmäler* ii pl. 27.1] need not be Eros. Coins with galloping winged horsemen, 78–55 BC, Sydenham, pl. 24.843, 870, 872, 874. For Protarchos, Vollenweider, 23–5, pls 12–3.

62 (127) Sardonyx cameo, white on brown. 17.5 mm. Flat back.
Seated Hermaphrodite uncovering her erection.
Formerly in the Marlborough Collection, Story-Maskelyne no. 136.
Replicas are *Berlin* 11241, fig., in glass; Babelon, *Camées* pl. 7.50; Paris, Chabouillet no. 44; at Pompeii, *Monumenti antichi* 1898, 334, fig. 43. Compare Vollenweider, pls 12.5, 13.5 for the drapery and Hermaphrodite figure. Hermaphrodites with erection are rare and this type is not noticed in Delcourt, *Hermaphroditea*. On a different group with a satyr see now Karageorghis, *Sculptures from Salamis* i no. 21.

63 (107) Nicolo cameo. 12 mm. Flat back.
Eros leans on an upturned torch.

Formerly in the Evans Collection [no. 115, pl. 11].
On the motif see Rumpf in *Reallexikon für Antike und Christentum* vi 333, 336.

64 (47) Sardonyx cameo, yellowish white on pale brown. 16 mm. Flat back.
Eros raises his hands to catch a butterfly.
Impronti dell'Istituto II.B 250.
For this gesture with the butterfly: *AG* iii 291, fig. 147, pl. 29.34 [Lippold, pl. 30.1].

65 (59) Sardonyx cameo, white on pale brown. 18 mm. Flat back.
A crouching Aphrodite wringing out her hair.
On the type see Lullies, *Die kauernde Aphrodite*. For the type in Egypt, Adriani, *Repertorio* A. ii 27–9, pls 60–1; the Rhodes statue, Lullies-Hirmer, *Greek Sculpture* ² pl. 273.

66 (53) Onyx cameo, white on dull grey. 13 mm.
Laureate head, possibly of Tiberius (reigned AD 14–37).
Formerly in the Beckford Collection.
The receding hair would suit a portrait of Nerva (reigned AD 96–8) but the nose is not sufficiently hooked. The Adam's apple is unusually prominent for Tiberius.

67 (60) Sardonyx cameo, white on palest brown. 15.5 mm.
A woman seated with a swaddled child on her knee.
Formerly in the Lherie, Roger de Sivry and Robinson [no. 33, pl.] Collections.
Compare the woman undressing a child on the cameo, *London* 3640, pl. 42.

68 (16) Sardonyx cameo, white on translucent brown. 21 mm. Flat back.
A woman preceded by a little girl carrying a torch and a jug.
Formerly in the Arundel and Marlborough [i pl. 43, Story-Maskelyne no. 603] Collections.

69 (19) Chalcedony cameo, pale blue on pale brown. 24 mm. Flat back.
Facing heads of a maenad and a bearded satyr, both wreathed with ivy.
A similar pair on the cameo, *Berlin* 11070, pl. 65.

70 (20) Sardonyx cameo, pink on brown. 13 mm. The back is flat, unpolished, white.
Facing head of a maenad, ivy-wreathed.
Formerly in the Rosarena Collection. *BFAC* pl. 112.O 59.
For this type compare *Berlin* 11070, pl. 65.

71 (132) Sardonyx cameo, pale brown on brown. 29 mm. Shallow convex back.
Four masks, two satyric, two tragic. Between them the name ΕΥΡΙΠΙΔΗC.
Formerly in the Hertz Collection. *AG* pl. 50.54.
The same composition of masks with 'HELENA' on the intaglios, *AG* pl. 65.17

101

[Marlborough Collection, Story-Maskelyne no. 671; Lippold, pl. 61.16] and *London* (Dalton) 899, pl. 33 (an eighteenth-century copy).

72 (18) Sardonyx cameo, white on very pale brown. 20.5 mm. Flat back.
A stork.
Formerly in the Hamilton Collection.
For similar creatures in pairs see *London* 3682, pl. 37; *Berlin* 7066, pl. 53; Smith and Hutton, *Catalogue of the Wyndham Francis Cook Collection* ii pl. 18.355 (with a nest).

73 (93) Sardonyx cameo, white on bluish brown. 25 mm. Chipped back.
Three-quarter head of Medusa with wings in her hair and snakes knotted beneath her chin.
For the type see Buschor, *Medusa Rondanini* 23 f., pl. 28.

74 (56) Nicolo cameo, pale blue on deep blue. 11 mm.
Leda and the swan.

75 (104) Sardonyx cameo, palest brown on white on brown. 23 mm.
A seated woman plays the double pipes. Before her the figure of Eros on a base, as a statuette. Behind her a pillar. Highly polished.
Formerly in the Robinson Collection [no. 34, pl.].

76 (22) Sardonyx cameo, dull white on pale milky brown. 14.5 mm. Flat back, unpolished.
Eros seated on the ground with a lyre. Summary style.
Formerly in the Robinson Collection [no. 90, pl.] and perhaps originally the Arundel and Marlborough Collections, Story-Maskelyne no. 155.
For this version see Gori i pl. 81.5 [Reinach, pl. 39]; Kassel, *Arch. Anzeiger* 1965, 65, no. 32; Musée Fol pl. 19.3.

77 (80) Cornelian cameo. 17 mm. Flat back.
High-relief mask of a bald head.
Formerly in the Marlborough Collection, Story-Maskelyne no. 670 (?)
Compare the plasma relief in Vienna, Eichler-Kris, *Kameen* pl. 61.522 (as seventeenth-century).

78 (112) Agate cameo, clear with a brown patch. 25.5 mm. Flat back and background.
A ram's head in relief.
Compare the lion-head relief in Vienna, Eichler-Kris, *Kameen* pl. 18.109.

79 (123) Agate cameo. 35 mm. Flat back, very shallow relief.
A hand pinches an ear. Around it a knotted diadem or necklace. Inscribed MNHMO-NEYE MOY THC KAΛHC ΨYXHC EYTYXI CΩΦPONI(E).

Formerly in the Marlborough [Story-Maskelyne no. 643] and Evans [no. 139, pl. 10] Collections.

Similar, equally elaborate gems are *London* 3694, fig. 79 and 3707, fig. 84; and for the long inscriptions see Babelon, *Camées* 187ff., and Carapanos Collection, *Journ. Int. d'Arch. Numismatique* xv (1913) pl. 14.949.

80 (73) Garnet ringstone. 18 mm. Flat face and back with bevelled edges.
A youth with a light beard rests against a pillar. A cloak beneath his arm and a stick in his right (in impression) hand with a snake around it. Ground line. Inscribed CΩTPATOY. Highly polished.
Formerly in the Rosarena Collection.
Compare the pose of the figure on *New York* 276, pl. 40 and p. 69. For other signatures 'Sotratou' see Brunn, *Geschichte der griechischen Künstler* ii 585 f.; Marlborough Collection, Story-Maskelyne no. 329 (Bellerophon); *London* (Dalton) 189, pl. 4.

81 (102) Mottled white jasper ringstone. 21.5 mm. Convex face and back.
A young man shoulders the body of a calf. Below the ground line the signature MOCXOY.
Formerly in the Morrison [no. 70, pl.] and Robinson [no. 60, pl.] Collections. See under *no. 48*.

82 (37) Chalcedony ringstone. 15.5 mm. Flat face and back, with bevelled edges.
Poseidon, shouldering his trident, rides a hippocamp. A dolphin beneath.
Formerly in the Poniatowsky Collection (?). Lippold, pl. 5.6 (as cornelian).
For the hippocamp biga on coins of *c.* 70 BC: Sydenham, pl. 23.796 A. Sixth-century Nereus: Beazley, *Attic Black Figure Vase Painters* 381.

83 (92) Agate intaglio. 26 mm. Flat face with bevelled sides.
Seated woman with a lyre. She wears a chiton. Ground line.
Formerly in the Fould and Rosarena Collections. Mentioned in *AG* ii, under pl. 14.19.
Another copy of this type, *AG* pl. 14.19; and compare *London* 604 [*AG* pl. 14.21] and Lippold, pl. 132.8, signed L. Pichler, showing the figure with a scroll, the lyre on an altar.

84 (88) Cornelian ringstone. 13.5 mm. Flat face and back with bevelled edges.
Leda and the swan. Ground line.
Impronti dell'Istituto Cades 2.I.A 137.
For this group compare *London* 1283, pl. 18; *AG* pl. 42.21.

85 (117) Garnet ringstone. 10 mm. Flat face.
Man's head. Inscribed M. ANTONIUS. Eighteenth century. Handlist–'by Dubarry or Guay'.

86 (41) Amethyst ringstone. 21 mm. Convex face, low-domed back. The surface is artificially roughened.
Three heads: the nearest laureate, the next that of a woman (?), the third a youth with his hair brushed back and caught in a fillet.
Impronti dell' Istituto A 72.
A similar sard, once in the Muirhead Collection, shown in King, *Ancient Gems and Rings* ii pl. 47.6 with pp. ix, xii ('brought from Egypt many years ago, and long in the possession of a noble lady') and *Handbook* pl. 70.2 ('found in India'); impression in Oxford. Edfu sealings with three heads, *Journal of Hellenic Studies* xxxvi (1916) pls 4.40, 5.224.

87 (57) Topaz ringstone. 18 mm. Flat face and back with bevelled edges.
Bust from a herm, with a bearded head wearing a twisted fillet of two strands and with butterfly wings attached behind the ears.
Formerly in the Rosarena Collection.
See *AG* iii 292f., on the type as Hermes as god of sleep, rather than Hypnos. Other examples with the angular wings: *Berlin* 6528, pl. 46; *London* 1957, pl. 25.

88 (78) Cornelian ringstone. 17 mm. Shallow convex face and back.
Mask wearing a vine wreath.
Lippold, pl. 153.1, as by L. Pichler.

89 (46) Amethyst ringstone. 22 mm. Convex face and back.
Bust of a youth with long hair. Highly polished.
Formerly in the Rosarena Collection.

90 (94) Pale cornelian ringstone. 23.5 mm.
Bust of a youthful Dionysos with ivy wreath.
Formerly in the Rosarena Collection.

91 (50) Garnet ringstone. 13.5 mm. Convex face and flat back. The surface is artificially roughened.
Three-quarter facing bust of a young satyr with a floral crown.
Formerly in the Lord Chesterfield, Bessborough and Marlborough Collections [Story-Maskelyne no. 210] (?)

92 (48) Plasma ringstone. 12 mm. Flat face.
Frontal face of a satyr crowned with ivy.
In this style the eighteenth-century gems, Lippold, pl. 153.9; *London* (Dalton) 737, pl. 26.

93 (61) Agate ringstone. 12.5 mm. High convex face, flat back with bevelled edges.
Facing mask of Pan with a vine wreath.

94 (85) Cornelian ringstone. 20.5 mm. Convex face, flat back.
Drunken satyr with wreath, thyrsos and jug, accompanied by a panther. Ground line.
Formerly in the Rosarena Collection.
Replica of the eighteenth-century gem with the signature ΣΚVMNOV [Lippold, pl. 108.3; Kibaltchitch Sale, Drouot, 27.iv. 1905 no. 169, pl.].

95 (26) Nicolo ringstone. 22 mm. Bevelled face, flat back.
A maenad dances, holding a kantharos and two-ended thyrsos, her head thrown back. At her side a panther and hanging in the field cymbals.
Two-ended thyrsoi on Campana reliefs, Rohden-Winnefeld, 40 fig. 66, pl. 101.2 and cf. pls 1 and 2.2; carried by a dancing satyr with kantharos and panther, as on our gem, on the New York relief, Richter, *Ancient Italy* fig. 204; cf. von Papen, *Der Thyrsos* 29, δίθυρσον.

96 (44) Topaz ringstone. 14 mm. Convex face and back.
Dionysos holding a thyrsos and kantharos. Ground line.
Some ancient models for this type: *AG* ii 121, pls 24.42, 25.23; *New York* 145, pl. 25 and p. 144.

97 (72) Agate ringstone. 14.5 mm. Flat face and back with bevelled edges.
Heads of a girl and a boar joined.

98 (91) Sardonyx cameo, white on mottled brown with a thin white layer towards the back. 29 mm. Convex back, pierced lengthways.
Facing head of Medusa with wings in her hair, snakes knotted beneath her chin.

99 (97) Sardonyx cameo, white between two yellow-brown layers. 14.5 mm. Flat back.
Kneeling Eros fights a cock, in a setting of gold with niello inlay.

THE FOLLOWING GEMS IN THE IONIDES COLLECTION ARE NOT ILLUSTRATED IN THIS BOOK:

100 (105) Green steatite scarab, v-winglets.
A cat. Egyptian.

101 (13) Chalcedony scarab. 10.5 mm. Simple beetle with light double ridge between the elytra.
Kneeling hawk-headed deity holding two feathers and wearing the crown of Lower Egypt. Ground line and line border. Phoenician (?), sixth-century BC.

102 (99) Blue chalcedony duck. 22 mm.
Formerly in the Strangford Collection. Lajard, *Culte de Venus* pl. 22.9.
Winged demon wearing horned cap, holding cone and bucket, with a fish body below the waist. Neo-Babylonian, sixth-century BC.

103 (101) Blue chalcedony cone. Height 26 mm, width 22 mm. Circular convex face.
Ahuramazda, crowned and holding a flower, in a disc surmounted by a crescent.
Around the disc four winged lions, their heads turned back.
Achaemenid, fifth century BC.

104 (130) Amygdaloid of pale green translucent steatite. 17 mm. The sides rather flattened.
A. A bull with head lowered and turned, as Boardman, *Island Gems* pl. 1.4, and by the same artist. Above its back a severed foreleg [cf. *ibid.*, pl. 10.299]. About 600 BC. Part broken away.
B. A bull with head lowered and turned. Cut later than A and possibly not in antiquity.

105 (7) Cornelian scarab. 16 mm. The beetle has a worn back, hatched border to the thorax, and plain legs and vertical border.
A high-footed volute crater in a hatched border. This may be a Greek scarab, recut in early Roman times with a fresh device, leaving traces of the original border.
Formerly in the Forman and Robinson [no. 11] Collections.

106 (49) Garnet ringstone. 19 mm. Convex face and shallow concave back.
Bearded head of Hermes, laureate and wearing a diminutive petasos.

107 (64) Pale cornelian ringstone. 12 mm. Flat face, convex back.
Bearded head wearing a fillet. Unpolished. Possibly modern.

108 (121) Garnet ringstone. 8 mm. Flat face.
Head of Apollo imitating the Roman Republican coin types of *c*. 90 BC. Probably modern.

109 (129) Nicolo ringstone. 13.5 mm. Flat face with bevelled sides, flat back with bevelled edges.
Fortuna holding a cornucopia and corn stalks. A steering oar beside her. Summary work.

110 (124) Chalcedony ringstone. 12.5 mm. Flat face with bevelled sides.
Standing woman with a staff and bird. A branch before her. Summary style. Second century AD.

106

111 (10) Cornelian ringstone. 13.5 mm. Convex face and back with bevelled edges. Ceres or Abundantia holding ears of corn and a tray of fruit. Summary style. Second century AD.

112 (84) Cornelian ringstone. 10.5 mm. Flat face, bevelled back.
Bust of Athena wearing a helmet with a wreath and an owl in relief on the crown. Not polished in the intaglio. Probably modern.

113 (108) Pale cornelian ringstone. 14.5 mm. Low convex face, flat back.
An old bald satyr, tailless, plays double pipes to a young satyr holding thyrsos and jug in the pose of our *no. 31*. Ground line. Possibly modern.

114 (29) Nicolo ringstone. 8.5 mm. Bevelled face, flat back.
A satyr dances, his head thrown back. Over one arm an animal skin and in the other hand a thyrsos. An overturned crater on the ground. Short ground line.
Formerly in the Rosarena Collection.
On this very common type, Vollenweider, 19, n. 20.

115 (28) Nicolo ringstone. 13 mm. Bevelled face, flat back.
Conversation between two youths with cloaks. One has his foot raised on a rock, his hand to his chin.
Formerly in the Rosarena Collection.

116 (55) Garnet ringstone. 7.5 mm. Convex face and back.
Facing head of Medusa, with wings in the hair and snakes knotted beneath the chin. Summary version of the Hellenistic type.

117 (126) Cornelian ringstone. 11 mm. Convex face, flat back with bevelled edges.
A pot with corn stalks being eaten by two mice. In the field an overturned pot.

118 (17) Sardonyx cameo, dull white on pale brown. 10.5 mm. Very rough-cut background and back.
A stag; replica of our *no. 11*. Ground line. Perhaps not ancient.
Formerly in the Robinson Collection [no. 31]. *BFAC* pl. 111. M 149.

119 (54) Chalcedony cameo, dull white on pale blue. 16 mm. Flat back.
Head of Apollo (?) with a lyre set before the neck.

120 (58) Mottled green stone cameo. 18 mm. Flat back.
Facing Medusa head with wings over the hair and snakes tied beneath the chin. Probably modern.

121 (110) Sardonyx cameo, white on brown. 24 mm. Flat back with bevelled edges. Head of a man.

122 (106) Gold ring. Length of bezel 13 mm. Octagonal bezel.
Facing head with wild hair. Inscribed around in Lombardic capitals ✠ R + ANDREA·
D·TONO * Italian, fourteenth–fifteenth century.

123 (11) Cornelian scaraboid. 18.5 mm. The convex back carries the device.
A four-winged goddess wearing a uraeus crown and holding flowers, standing above
a lotus. Probably modern.
Formerly in the Evans Collection [no. 45, pl. 3].

Other gems recorded as being once in the Ionides Collection include *AG* pl. 38.28, and
pl. 65.30 [Marlborough Collection, Story-Maskelyne no. 57].

BIBLIOGRAPHY

ABBREVIATIONS

ACKNOWLEDGEMENTS

INDEXES

BIBLIOGRAPHY AND ABBREVIATIONS

Furtwängler's *Die antiken Gemmen* (1900) remains the only comprehensive account of ancient gem-engraving, but parts of it are superseded by later studies. For the early Roman period the most important works are Miss M.L. Vollenweider's *Die Steinschneiderkunst* (1966) and *Gemmenporträts der Römischen Republik* (1967). On materials see G.F. Herbert Smith, *Gem Stones* (1949) and for Pliny's account, S.H. Ball, *A Roman Book on Precious Stones* (1950). Of the catalogues which appear in the list below the most informative are those devoted to the collections in Berlin, London, New York and Lewes House (now in Boston). A number of new monographs and catalogues are due to appear in the near future.

ABBREVIATIONS

AG	Furtwängler, *Die antiken Gemmen* (1900)
Berlin	Furtwängler, *Beschreibung der geschnittenen Steine im Antiquarium, Berlin* (1896)
BFAC	*The Burlington Fine Art Club, Exhibition of Greek Art* (1904)
Evans	*Pierres gravées antiques: collection d'un archéologue-explorateur.* Vente, Hôtel Drouot, 8 May 1905
LHG	Beazley, *The Lewes House Collection of Ancient Gems* (1920)
Lippold	Lippold, *Gemmen und Kameen* (1922)
London	Walters, *Catalogue of the Engraved Gems and Cameos* (1926)
London (Dalton)	Dalton, *Catalogue of the Engraved Gems of the post-classical periods in the British Museum* (1915)
Marlborough	Plate references are to *Gemmarum antiquarum delectus; ex praestantioribus desumptus, quae in dactyliothecis ducis Marlburensis conservantur* (1780–91). Catalogue numbers refer to Story-Maskelyne, *The Marlborough Gems* (1870)
Morrison	Sale Catalogue. Christies, 29 June 1898

111

New York	Richter, *Catalogue of Engraved Gems, Metropolitan Museum of Art, New York* (1956)
Reinach	Reinach, *Pierres gravées* (1895). Repeats the illustrations of the Marlborough catalogue and others
Robinson	Sale Catalogue. Christies, 22 June 1909
Rohden-Winnefeld	Rohden and Winnefeld, *Architektonische römische Tonreliefs* (1911)
Sydenham	Sydenham, *The Coinage of the Roman Republic* (1952)
Vollenweider	Vollenweider, *Die Steinschneiderkunst und ihre Künstler in spät-republikanischer und augusteischer Zeit* (1966)

ACKNOWLEDGEMENTS

I have to thank various scholars whose advice I have sought in preparing this book: notably Miss Vollenweider, who has not seen the stones and cannot therefore be held responsible for any attributions here suggested; Bernard Ashmole, Peter Fraser, Martin Robertson, Gerald Taylor, Stefan Weinstock.

INDEXES

I MOTIFS

II INSCRIPTIONS

III ARTISTS AND OTHER SUBJECTS